Swarthmore Lecture 1992

£8.50

AND SILENCE

The future of Quaker ministry

by
Brenda Clifft Heales
and Chris Cook

QUAKER HOME SERVICE

First published May 1992

This book is copyright under the Berne Convention. Apart
from any fair dealing for the purposes of private study,
research, criticism or review, as permitted under the
Copyright Act 1956, no portion may be reproduced without
written permission. Inquiries should be addressed to the
Secretary, Swarthmore Lecture Committee, c/o Quaker Home
Service, Friends House, Euston Road, London NW1 2BJ.

© Chris Cook and Brenda Clifft Heales

ISBN 0 85245 242 X

Cover design by John Blamires from a traditional Amish
quilted bag supplied by the authors.

Acknowledgements
The authors and Quaker Home Service gladly make
acknowledgements to the writers and publishers listed in the
bibliography who have been quoted in this book. Every
endeavour has been made to trace the sources of quotations
and obtain permission, but where this has not been possible,
we apologise for any unintentional breach of copyright.

Printed in Great Britain

Preface

The Swarthmore Lectureship was established by the Woodbrooke Extension Committee at a meeting held December 9, 1907: the minute of the Committee providing for an 'annual lecture on some subject relating to the message and work of the Society of Friends'. The name Swarthmore was chosen in memory of the home of Margaret Fox, which was always open to the earnest seeker after Truth, and from which loving words of sympathy and substantial material help were sent to fellow workers.

The lectureship has a twofold purpose: first, to interpret to the members of the Society of Friends their message and mission; and secondly, to bring before the public the spirit, the aims and fundamental principles of Friends. The lecturers alone are responsible for any opinions expressed.

The lectureship provides both for the publication of a book and for the delivery of a lecture, the latter usually at the time of assembly of London Yearly Meeting of the Society of Friends. A lecture related to the present book was delivered at Friends House, Euston Road, London, on the evening of May 23rd, 1992.

CONTENTS

FOREWORD

The subject suggested to us for the Swarthmore Lecture 1992 was "ministry". We were invited to begin by considering ministry in Meeting for Worship in London Yearly Meeting of the Religious Society of Friends, and then, if so moved, to consider ministry among Friends other than in Meeting for Worship, in other Yearly Meetings, other Quaker traditions, or even other religious traditions. As it finally came together, the shape of the book is not unlike what the Swarthmore Lecture Committee first suggested.

Our title *Images and Silence* reflects our interest in the two main approaches to God which appear in traditional theology. Brenda has written about the relationship between images, religious experience and worship, and Chris about the imageless aspect of God described by some mystics. We do not regard these as being opposed to one another; they are two sides of the same coin, or two views of the same mountain. Nor are we suggesting a choice has to be made between them. In fact, such a choice is impossible, as both operate in different ways at different times in our lives. An image might come to us in our reading, in prayer, or in worship, which leads us into absolute imagelessness. Or, during meditation or contemplative prayer we may seem to have entered the place of utmost emptiness, and then suddenly be aware of images charged with energy and significance.

There being two writers (a 'first' in the history of the Swarthmore Lecture) caused some technical problems, notably of 'voice'—which of us is speaking when, and does *we* stand for the writers, or the Religious Society of Friends of which we are members? Some of the book is jointly written (Parts I and IV). Here we often refer to Friends in the third person plural, while *we* usually means the two writers. Sometimes we have, how-

1

ever, used phrases like 'we Friends' or 'we all', because we wanted to emphasise our sense of belonging to the Society of Friends; any criticism we make of *them* is also criticism of *us*. Never have we felt any sense of separation from any of the problems described, even when we were under the constraint of writing in a detached style. Part II was written by Brenda alone, Part III by Chris alone, and there are thus no problems of 'voice' in these chapters.

We are united in our belief that Meeting for Worship is the soul of Quakerism, and that the soul's health determines quality of life, and that from the life flows ministry, wherever it is offered.

Finally we have deeply felt thanks to give to all who have helped us: family and friends and Friends, both in this country—specially our two helpers on the Swarthmore Lecture Committee, Beth Allen and Elisabeth Salisbury, and Friends in Purley and Sutton Monthly Meeting (and specially Helen Drewery and Gerald Moss)—and at Pendle Hill Quaker Centre for Study and Contemplation in Pennsylvania, where we were happy guests during the miraculously sunny Fall of 1991. From all these friends and many others we received loving support, encouragement and criticism, all (as Mary Elson said in 1686) 'knit and tyed and bundled up' with humour. This book would have been impossible without them.

PART I

MINISTRY TODAY

Centre Diamond

On the cover of this book is a design based on a piece of Amish quilting. The Amish are one of the historic peace churches, and split from the Mennonites at the end of the seventeenth century. There are groups of them in parts of North America who still 'dress plain' and retain many of their original traditions, eschewing modern technology and energy sources. There are many Amish farming in Lancaster County, Pennsylvania, and we spent a day there during our term at Pendle Hill, trying to get some sense of their present lives.

The design of the quilting shown on the cover, called 'diamond in the centre', is traditional, as are the colours. Connections could be made with the Buddhist symbol of the jewel in the heart of the lotus, and with Jesus's image of the Kingdom of Heaven as a pearl of great price. The colours recall and suggest earth's plenitude, and the surrounding black the formlessness from which the creation emerged.

The image contained in the design is, however, not representational. We have chosen it for our cover because, in its near abstraction, as nearly abstract as an image can be, it points towards imagelessness and silence.

To gaze at this image is to experience stillness. The archetypal shapes, in their rich yet sombre colours, seem to have authority, emptying the mind of its normal clutter of semi-conscious, half-acknowledged thoughts, bringing one's whole being into deep, steady awareness, into sacred space.

CHAPTER 1

What is Ministry?

A man was going down from Jerusalem to Jericho, and he fell among robbers, who stripped him and beat him, and departed, leaving him half-dead. Now by chance a priest was going down that road; and when he saw him he passed by on the other side. So likewise a Levite, when he came to the place and saw him, passed by on the other side. But a Samaritan, as he journeyed, came to where he was; and when he saw him, he had compassion, and went to him and bound up his wounds, pouring on oil and wine; then he set him on his own beast and brought him to an inn, and took care of him. And the next day he took out two denarii and gave them to the inn-keeper, saying, 'Take care of him; and whatever more you spend, I will repay you when I come back.'[1]

* * *

Brenda: Painting in watercolour is one of the ways in which I experience ministry. My everyday occupations drop away and the mosquito mind stops buzzing.

As I work my concentration intensifies, focusing on shapes, colours and the way the paint moves on the paper. It is guided by me but it is also mysteriously itself in the wonderful capacity of water to defy boundaries and then make its own. I interact with it in a relationship of control and freedom, power and deep respect. Because I love this activity I empty myself into it and in this self-forgetting I experience a healing, nurturing presence.

When I finish there are always aspects of the painting which are frustrating and disappointing; but unless I am very unlucky something has worked well. The energy I spent is now beamed back: the picture is both me and not me. I painted it, but something not in my conscious control was also involved. Like my children, who were part of my body before birth, the picture now has its own independent life.

The love which the action of painting released has changed me, made me more whole. I hope that something of that love and wholeness can be communicated to other people.

*   *   *

Chris: I love calligraphy—both seeing it and practising it: something to do with the pure line in an apt curve on the beautiful paper— the simpler the better. Its ministry to me is to centre me, by combining beauty, rightness and concentration.

*   *   *

'At approximately 2.00 a.m. on Friday, February 24, 1989, United Airlines flight 811 took off from Honolulu, Hawaii, destined for New Zealand. The Boeing 747 jumbo jet was climbing through an altitude of 22,000 feet, when suddenly there was a violent shudder of the fuselage. A loud crash followed, and the huge plane leaned to the left. The cockpit crew was unaware at the time that the forward cargo door of the jet had been blown open, tearing a huge 10-foot by 25-foot hole in the side of the plane. Nine passengers were sucked out of the plane to their deaths. . . .

'Captain Cronin, a veteran of thirty-eight years of military and commercial flying, put all his knowledge and experience on the line. . . .

'His stickiest problem . . . was deciding how fast to fly. Captain Cronin slowed the plane as close to the stall speed as possible to keep the air rushing over the plane from further widening the hole in the fuselage. Because the hole had changed the aerodynamics of the huge craft, the usual data regarding stall speed was no longer relevant. The pilot had to use his best judgement.

'Furthermore, since the plane had just taken on 300,000 pounds of fuel for the long flight, it was too heavy to land without collapsing the landing gear. Captain Cronin began dumping fuel at the maximum rate, but quickly calculated he would still be above the recommended weight for landing unless he circled the island. Fearing that the hole in the fuselage might widen, he decided to risk landing overweight.

'But then he encountered a new problem. The wing flaps used to slow the plane down were not working properly. He would have to land the plane at a higher than recommended speed.

'Captain Cronin headed the plane for the longest runway at Honolulu airport. He would have to land the plane at 195 miles per hour, compared to the normal speed of 170 miles per hour. The jet weighed 610,000 pounds, well above Boeing's recommended maximum stress load of 564,000 pounds. Nevertheless, Captain Cronin made one of the smoothest landings the rest of the crew could remember, amid the cheers of the passengers. . . .

'A few days after the harrowing experience, an interviewer asked Captain Cronin about his first thoughts following the loss of the cargo door. He said, 'I said a prayer for my passengers momentarily and then got back to business.'[2]

*   *   *

Chris: The ministry of the word—in a book. The book that changed my life most radically was W.H. Vanstone's *Love's Endeavour, Love's Expense*, which released me from the omnipotent Old Man With a Beard and offered a God who in pure love cannot determine outcomes or falsify consequences—

only suffer with us and work with more energy and self-giving than we can begin to imagine, to bring the best out of all that happens. That saved my faith.[3]

*   *   *

An important ministry undertaken by Margaret Fell in the seventeenth century was writing pamphlets and letters. She wrote to persecutors of Friends, passionately denouncing their actions; she corresponded with "priests and professors", explaining the inward, experiential nature of Quakerism; she wrote to many imprisoned Friends letters of comfort and support in their suffering; to travelling Quaker ministers her letters were so important that they replied thanking her for the help received both for them and their families and begging her for her prayers. Above all they implored her to continue to write to them, their 'dear counsellor and comforter' as John Stubbs called her in 1657.

*   *   *

A Friend in 1992 writes to a prisoner on Death Row in a North American Prison. Others do the same. Sometimes this saves a prisoner's sanity—certainly self-respect. It is the caring for a complete stranger that breaks through.

*   *   *

Chris: At my very first Yearly Meeting, in London in the 1970s, a Friend who had been abroad for some years rose and asked why none of us any longer had time to spare for one another: why were we too busy to listen? I have never forgotten this, and it has made a real difference to how I try to order my life.

*   *   *

William Wordsworth:

. . . That best portion of a good man's life,

His little, nameless, unremembered acts
Of kindness and of love.[4]

*   *   *

There is a scheme, PAT, which takes dogs into hospitals and hospices for patients to stroke.

Eighty-five per cent of people in a survey in North Wales feed the birds in the winter.

*   *   *

Brenda: Once I was part of a group which was asked: Which two aspects of Quakerism have so much value for you that their loss would mean you could no longer be a Friend?

My answer came immediately: Meeting for Worship and being in a loving community. My Meeting is my extended family; it supports me, nurtures me, laughs at and with me, and accepts me with all my shortcomings. It is a community of love and a cell of strength.

*   *   *

In Meeting for Worship, an elder who frequently ministered at length and in long sentences, one Sunday simply said, 'I was washing up, and suddenly saw the meniscus on a cup brimming with water. I was filled with joy at its perfection.'

In Meeting for Worship, a Friend cried because a teenage pupil had spat at her in school that week.

In Meeting for Worship, a gathered silence.

*   *   *

'To minister is to serve, and to each Christian community comes the call, "By love serve one another".' This is not a call to a self-sufficient or self-preoccupied community life, but to one where the spirit of loving service naturally extends to those around it.

The earlier part of this chapter is concerned with the vocal ministry in our meetings for worship. But our understanding of ministry is not limited to this aspect. We have known in our meetings a ministry of silence by which we sustain and strengthen one another. There is also a ministry of caring one for another, and the latter part of this chapter is concerned with this aspect of our family life. In this life it is for each to discover and exercise his own gift: 'As every man hath received the gift, even so minister the same one to another, as good stewards of the manifold grace of God.'[5]

* * *

In writing this book we have had in mind all these kinds of ministry. We are aware that the concept of service is a fundamental framework within which ministry lives and has its being. We are deeply aware that serving the needs of the world—caring for one another in this sense—is one of the most important traditions of Christianity in general and the Religious Society of Friends in particular. Friends have always tried to respond to the world's needs, working for peace and justice, feeding the poor, and seeking other ways to relieve suffering. It is heartening that much of this work goes ahead whatever the circumstances, and that many of our resources as a religious body are channelled into these areas of concern.

It is our belief, however, that the attention of Friends as a religious body needs to focus also on the other aspects of ministry. We feel that these have been somewhat marginalised, if not neglected, and therefore an important aim of this book is to focus attention on them.

We are aware that our own reflections are, inevitably, personal, and that our perspectives on ministry cannot be comprehensive. We have tried, however, to listen to what is being said by Friends. The kinds of experience we have found valuable in this respect have included our term as Friends-in-Residence at Woodbrooke (Quaker) College in the Autumn of 1990, where we taught a course on the subject of ministry, and also our work with Appleseed, which is in itself one form of ministry.[6]

We had further insights into ministry, among North American Friends, when we were Friends-in-Residence at Pendle Hill Quaker Centre for Study and Contemplation, in Pennsylvania, for the Autumn Term of 1991.

We begin, however, by referring in some detail to a conference held at Woodbrooke and Westhill Colleges in 1990. Called *Equipping for Ministry*, it was a very large national conference whose theme was "To consider how Friends can help each other to discover their sense of calling today and nurture the various gifts of ministry which are present among them."[7] We begin here because as many Friends have commented, what happened at this conference showed more clearly than anything else could the pulse of London Yearly Meeting of the Religious Society of Friends in the last decade of the twentieth century.

The conference was to address three questions in particular:

1. What is the Quaker understanding of ministry in all its forms? (in worship, in the life of the meeting, and in the world around us).
2. How do we best minister to each other?
3. How can we provide resources and opportunities to nurture ministry?

The first question asked for some thoughtful analysis; it demanded breadth of consideration and the need to think philosophically, in the sense of being aware of definitions. The second question is the most personal and experiential, while the third asks for a planning strategy to meet future needs.

Some participants were sent by their Meetings, each Monthly Meeting having been invited to do this. Other participants had applied privately, so to speak. Other churches were invited to send observers, and did so.

What actually happened was that instead of the conference exploding outwards into ideas, insights and suggestions in response to the three questions, it imploded, showing a deep, persistent concern with healing and nurturing the inner life, especially the inner life of the conference participants.

It has been observed by organisers of other courses and conferences that this 'implosion' is a common occurrence. There is a hidden agenda which participants bring to such courses and conferences, which relates to the desperate need felt by many to receive ministry for their own suffering. Many people come for personal rather than conceptual reasons—a sign of their unfulfilled needs.

There is a further point to be made about this particular conference, concerning the Meetings for Worship held during the course of it. Intervention by one of those responsible for the right holding of the meetings did not prevent the stream of ministry which flowed almost without pause as one cry of pain, or expression of anguish followed another. For some this gave a rare opportunity to be heard at last; for others there was the opportunity to reach out and hold in their love and prayers those who were experiencing so much darkness. For yet others, it was a travesty of a Meeting for Worship, allowing no time for the echoes of what had been said to subside before fresh voices were added, no time for the silence with its healing power to enter the darkness, no space to allow the Holy Spirit to break in: no real listening. In fact much (though not all) the spoken ministry seemed to be based on the assumption that no-one had been listening, was listening, or ever would listen. This gave considerable pain to both of us as we sat there, and to Brenda came T.S. Eliot's words:

The notion of some infinitely gentle,
Infinitely suffering thing.[8]

This image of God's infinite, gentle participation in the suffering, indeed identification with it, was extremely painful to experience in a situation where it seemed God was being brushed aside as irrelevant.

There is a marked contrast between the conference's way of dealing with pain in Meeting for Worship and Isaac Penington's view of the help given to the afflicted in worship:

> And if any be burthened, tempted, buffeted by Satan, bowed down, overborne, languishing, afflicted, distressed etc., the estate of such is felt in spirit, and secret cries, or open, as the Lord pleaseth, ascend up to the Lord for them: and they, many times find ease and relief in a few words spoken, or without words, if it be the season of their help and relief with the Lord.[9]

To sum up: this was a conference which was unable to pay attention in two senses; it was unable to pay attention to the theme and ideas, the conceptual framework, and it was unable to pay attention to God in worship.

These are significant failures, and they are connected. If Friends do not experience true ministry in Meeting for Worship, they are not able to do God's work, or to carry out God's ministry in the world. And 'the world' includes themselves, because they will not be empowered. *Church Government* concludes its sections on the ministry of the word by emphasising this necessary connection:

> The purpose of all ministry is to lead the meeting into a closer communion with God, and into a fresh vision of the purposes he would have us pursue as we seek his kingdom.[10]

Two phrases here seem specially significant:

'a closer communion with God'
'a fresh vision of (God's) purposes'

Are these really the reasons why we all come to Meeting for Worship on Sunday mornings? For Brenda the hopes and expectations while sinking into the gathering silence run something like this:

'I hope to feel God's presence and know God's will, but accompanying my hope is also dread that someone will rise yet again to tell us about the ecological crisis, or the arms trade, or about some terrible and unrelieved suffering. This makes me squirm in my seat in a state of arid guilt, fruitless frustration. I resent these facts, ideas and situations, now, in worship. I need the sense of immanence and a vision, so that I can act on myself and act in the world. I recognise that the world is damaged and its glory dimmed because, as Gerard Manley Hopkins said:

Generations have trod, have trod, have trod;
And all is seared with trade; bleared, smeared with toil

But I also need to feel, with Hopkins,

And for all this, nature is never spent;
There lives the dearest freshness deep down things;
And though the last lights off the black West went
Oh, morning, at the brown brink eastward, springs—
Because the Holy Ghost over the bent
World broods with warm breast and with ah! bright wings![11]

*　　*　　*

Do we Friends have experiences of God in Meeting for Worship which sustain us and empower us in the world outside? Are we so filled with the Holy Spirit in our worship that we feel that healing power within ourselves and for the needy world?

We believe that Friends' service to the world as a religious body, which is a ministry of healing and empowering of self and others, must spring from the Meeting for Worship, the communal experience of the presence of God.

CHAPTER 2

Meeting for Worship

In speaking of what they do on Sunday mornings most Friends use 'Meeting' as a convenient abbreviation for the more cumbersome 'Meeting for Worship', believing that this shorthand is only for ease of expression and that it does not signify any underlying ellipsis of meaning. It can, however, allow a slide into a situation where the sense or concept of worship is almost absent in attitudes to Meeting for Worship. If Friends go to Meeting 'with heart and mind prepared' for worship they will expect a difference in kind, in both the nature of the vocal ministry and the depth of the silence, from what might exist if they are expecting to share with others their feelings about personal crises or political or social concerns in an affable, but secular, framework.

What do Friends expect to happen when they worship? In *Church Government*, the first paragraph in the section on ministry is actually about the nature of worship.

> Worship is the response of the human spirit to the presence of the divine and eternal, to the God who first seeks us. The sense of wonder and awe of the finite creature before his creator cannot but lead to thanksgiving and adoration.[1]

It is instructive to see how what is said in *Church Government* relates to our actual Meetings for Worship on Sunday mornings. In our experience it is rare to find that the dominant atmosphere in a Meeting for Worship is a sense of wonder and awe, of thanksgiving and adoration. So is *Church Government* seriously outdated? Is it out of touch with what Meetings are really like? Or are Meetings out of touch with their true purpose? Or is the issue more complex than these questions suggest?

Is this concept of worship no longer relevant for our time? Our age is characterised by increasing secularization. It is intellectually dominated by the philosophy of logical positivism with its rejection of absolute moral concepts, and theologically confused by the polarization of liberal Christian humanism and the narrow certainties of the fundamentalist evangelical movement. We Friends have always viewed with suspicion any fixed and absolute concepts relating to belief and faith, and some of us now sit uneasily towards more traditional Quaker concepts of worship.

It seems that rather than focusing on awe and adoration, attention has been on bringing hurts and brokenness, ideas and opinions to Meeting, and sharing these in ministry. Meetings can then become either a sharing of anguish or a sharing of notions with little space for wonder and awe, thanksgiving and adoration. That there is such little space for these is true in two senses. First, the person ministering does not feel any of these emotions or responses; second, the Meeting as a whole does not provide a framework for them.

All too often the Meeting, instead of being a Meeting for Worship, can become something else: it can become Meeting for Counselling.

Many Friends seem to be unable to experience the feelings which are part of worship because other feelings are dominant. Their own suffering and grief and need for help are dominant. There is nothing unChristian or unQuakerly about that. The crowds who followed Jesus included many who came for healing, for specific physical healing and for the healing of psychological and social hurts. They came in faith and asked, or their friends and relations asked for them, or they reached out in faith, wordlessly, to touch the hem of Jesus's garment. They waited for the healing power. It seems that herein lies the difference. Much of the anguish expressed in Meetings seems to be not so much a cry to God, as a cry of despair which is being offered for therapy by the Meeting, an appeal to other members of the Meeting for support and acknowledgment.

This kind of spoken ministry can be deeply moving to all who hear, but it is also deeply disturbing for all if what follows is either another example of personal suffering, or attempts at counselling. What is implicit in this situation is that if most of the time no single person listens to us, then the only way of being heard is to address the captive audience of a silent Friends Meeting. However, this captive audience is not perceived to include God. So what seems to be happening in many Meetings is that individuals come who need to share their pain and have found no other way of being heard than during the silent Meeting. They come for the healing of their hurts, but they come with only an incomplete acceptance that the mystery of God's presence is at the heart of Meeting for Worship. Because their audience does not include God they don't listen for an answer, they don't allow the power of the Holy Spirit in a gathered Meeting to over-shadow them '. . . as a hen gathers her chicks under her wings'. If you don't believe God is present, what answer are you expecting and from whom?

What kind of ministry, what kind of nurturing do such individuals need? Three kinds, at least. Firstly, they need to be heard outside of Meeting, really listened to. One of the most healing acts we can do for each other is to concentrate, to pay attention. Prayer has been described by Iris Murdoch as 'an attention to God, which is a form of love'.[2] This can be extended by saying that paying attention to *anyone* is a form of love. It is one of the ways in which Friends can minister to each other. During our term at Woodbrooke we saw the expression of the same need in the seeking for spiritual friendship and co-counselling.

The second kind of nurturing needed is a framework for looking inwards, to examine inner darkness and personal needs so

17

that individual gifts can be discovered. This takes courage and is helped when there is a sense of being part of a supportive community, a community in which the individual faces are turned to the same light, a community in which individuals are going on a journey together.

Thirdly, we all have to learn to listen. We need to listen in a variety of ways: to practise listening to others, to experiences expressed in books, music and art, to ourselves. 'How do I know what I'm thinking until I hear what I say?', as E.M. Forster once asked. Above all, we need to listen to God.

If we all come to Meeting for Worship after having been heard, having been listened to by others, our need to unburden ourselves in Meeting will be less intense, and there will be less likelihood of Meeting for Worship being reduced to Meeting for Counselling. If we come expecting, hoping, believing that in Meeting we can approach God, then we come to Meeting as communicants in other churches come to God in the Eucharist:

> And here we offer and present unto thee, O Lord, ourselves, our souls and bodies, to be a reasonable, holy, and lively sacrifice unto thee; humbly beseeching thee, that all we, who are partakers of this holy Communion, may be fulfilled with thy grace and heavenly benediction.[3]

Friends' Meetings are their Holy Communion, and communion was in fact a word which seventeenth century Friends often used to describe Meeting for Worship. Friends' Eucharist, the bread and wine, are the words and the silence. We come bringing ourselves, our souls and bodies with all our troubles, joys, problems, confusions, to lay before God, praying for God's grace and blessing to fill us so that we may bear our sorrows and share our happiness. We come to God for the Holy Spirit to minister to us. Only then, after our healing and in our wholeness can we give ministry to others. If I am bankrupt I cannot give a donation to Oxfam, nor can I feed myself. If I am spiritually bankrupt I am correspondingly paralysed.

A great need for personal spiritual nurture is being expressed today, the need for the kind of support and help which will enable people to come to God in their troubles, and through God's help and the help of the community of Friends, to make the journey inwards, the experiment in depth.

It is, however, not only individuals who need such nurturing. The Meeting as a whole needs education in the experience of the things which are eternal. Meetings need to follow the basic disciplines: of allowing silence between spoken ministry; of paying attention to what is being said; of being sure there really is a call to minister before standing up and that it is not just an urge to share a good idea, or impress others, or even pass on some propaganda.

We are not suggesting that Friends should be careful to present a bland optimism to each other on Sunday mornings. There is much that is good if Friends are seen to be open and honest with their hurts and not hiding or suppressing them, either in relation to themselves or their Meeting. This kind of open sharing can be the first stage of self-discovery. It is far more worrying if people suffer and are silent, if pain festers beneath the surface, if fears are suppressed in order to present a cheerful face to the world. The same is true of Meetings, and the Meeting which hides and buries its hurts, where Friends fear to reveal the darker aspects of life, is likely to be dead inside.

There are times when it is right for pain, hurt and suffering to be brought into Meeting for Worship. This is when they are brought for God's healing.

Where can I go from your spirit?
Or where can I flee from your presence?
If I ascend to heaven, you are there;
If I make my bed in hell, behold, you are there.

If I take the wings of the morning
And dwell in the uttermost parts of the sea,
Even there your hand shall lead me,
And your right hand shall hold me.
If I say, 'Surely the darkness shall fall on me,'
Even the night shall be light about me;
Indeed the darkness shall not hide from you.
But the night shines as the day.
The darkness and the light are both alike to you.'[4]

Here hurt and pain are absorbed into mystery. Mystery, and a sense of the sacred, are broader, more encompassing terms than wonder, awe, thanksgiving and adoration, because they include a wider range of the experiences brought to Meeting for Worship. Hurt and pain should be shared in Meeting, not with a view to drawing attention to them, but because in the community's experience of God, healing can take place.

Meeting for Discussion is another way of not having Meeting for Worship. It is different from the outpourings of personal preoccupations in that it functions through notions and generalisations. It is, however, another major way in which we secularize our Meetings. Beth Allen, in *The Revolution is Here*[5] questions the characteristics of our Meetings and asks what distinguishes us from say, a ten-pin bowling club or over-sixties club. She continues:

A Meeting is a social group but if we are to make real the Kingdom of God for others today we must have more dynamic, more power, more centre than an amateur dramatic society or a gardening club.

For many Meetings these qualities of power and centredness are dissipated by flaccid discussion. During the Gulf war in 1990 some Meetings were more like a TV discussion programme or a radio phone-in than a Meeting for Worship. How can we Friends re-charge our batteries so that we can go out and do our peace-making, our reconciling, our protesting, if we do not plug ourselves into the source of power? If we don't plug ourselves into the Holy Spirit, where is our energy to come from? From our inner compulsions? Are these of God? How can we know if we never pause to ask or to listen? St. Teresa's dictum that God has no hands but ours is often quoted in ministry: but we will have no hands but our own unless we let ourselves 'stand still in the light, for then content comes'.[6]

Richard Bauman says:

Part of the Quakers' understanding of the efficacy of the spiritual ministry rested on their theory of communication and rhetorical power. They believed that the spiritual truth of a religious message stemmed from its source, God speaking within . . . Truth was felt to be the resonant chord struck within one's conscience by another's message.[7]

Robert Barclay describes truly powerful spoken ministry as coming from one who is really empowered,

'. . . being able to speak from a living experience of what he himself is a witness . . . his words and ministry, proceeding from the inward power and virtue, reach to the heart of his hearers, and make them approve of him, and be subject to him.'[8]

Now, this is not to elevate in a hierarchical sense one who ministers, which would be anathema to most Friends. It is to hear, to recognise in such ministry the voice of prophecy, the voice of God, coming through the agency, the channel of the Friend who speaks.

In the seventeenth century Friends thought ministry was like the sense of calling experienced by the apostles:

'They were called by power from on high, and were made

ministers by the gift of the Holy Spirit received from God, and their ministry was an absolute gift from God.'[9]

It is this sense of being in touch with spiritual power, this connection with the sacred, which is absent from the kind of ministry which deals in ideas about the solution to social and political ills.

What do we Friends think we are doing when we turn Meeting for Worship into Meeting for Discussion? Although Meeting for Discussion is different in many ways from Meeting for Counselling, both are aberrant forms of a Quaker Meeting. Neither has very much to do with worship. Again and again we hear the need for peace insistently and sometimes aggressively declaimed, the evil of war powerfully denounced, the awfulness of it all decried. We have even heard notices about protest or pressure group meetings, complete with date, time and place, given in Meeting for Worship as if they were ministry. Do Friends, or God, need to be convinced of such truths, let alone given such information as part of worship? George Fox denounced this kind of ministry which preaches to the converted and presents them with welcome concepts; in fact this procedure was described by seventeenth century Friends as 'ministering to the itching ear'.

Suppose, however, Friends *did* need persuading. Is Meeting for Worship the right place for this? Suppose Friends did need education and information on the facts of, say, the arms trade, precision bombing, opposing an act of aggression and the relation of all this to the Peace Testimony. Is Meeting for Worship the place where this kind of exercise should happen? We more properly see these issues examined and debated in *The Friend*, in informal discussion groups or at specially convened meetings and conferences.

What is seen here again is a lack of discipline; a treating of Meeting for Worship as a rag bag of needs, thoughts, ideas, concerns, a convenient forum where these can be shared and debated.

This is not to say, of course, that Friends' concerns and anxieties about political, economic or social issues should never appear in Meeting for Worship.

Sometimes ministry from a very deep inner spring will take the form of prophecy—the incisive word of God about a situation that needs spiritual surgery. Sometimes this will come from a well-informed Friend, and may well seem political at first. Yet the listener will soon hear something deeper than an opinion, something unexpected, uncomfortable or even angry. The Hebrew and Christian scriptures alike are clear that God gives priority to the widow, the orphan and the refugee, the poor and hungry, the grieving and sick. Because of this, what God has to say about these marginalised people (and issues) comes from a much hotter and more dangerous place than human opinions, however heated and contentious those might be. And we do, most of us, know the difference between the speaker's opinion and ministry that comes from the true source.

Richard Bauman distinguished two kinds of ministry which flourished among early Friends: mission and nurturing. These were clearly differentiated. Mission was involvement in the Lamb's war, to turn the world upside down by working in public places, in order to bring the truth before those who had not yet received it, to plough the ground and plant the seed of their new faith. Nurturing, on the other hand, was for those already responsive to the truth who sought out the Quaker ministers voluntarily for further spiritual assistance.[10]

In Friends' Meetings today these two kinds of ministry are seen, but with the following differences: firstly they tend to be conflated, and secondly they are sometimes secularized. Yet as T. Edmund Harvey says:

Unless we can feel that power in the ministry which comes

from the impact of eternity breaking in upon us, how can we make that supreme dedication which is needed if discipleship is to be real and effective?[11]

Our manner of worship is not easy. Quakerism has been described as a religion for mature people of a mystical disposition. Meeting for Worship is difficult in the demands it makes on each of us. Early Friends recognised this and also recognised the power which was generated by the tension between speaking and silence. The spiritual risk involved derived from the 'tension between the desire to give oneself up to God's will and the susceptibility to self-will that was part of the human condition'.[12] Guidance was given in relation to spoken ministry which included being certain that one had a motion and opening from God and that one's message was for others and not just for oneself, knowing when to begin and when to stop. There was also the danger of suppressing God's word because of doubts about the certainty of a true leading. The only final guidance was to wait in the silence, looking to the light within, laying aside the self and its flickering mental distractions, and paying that perfect attention to God which is complete mindfulness, pure contemplation.

> For if you sit still in the patience which overcomes in the power of God, there will be no flying. For the husbandman, after he hath sown his seed, he is patient. For by the power and by the light you will come to see through and feel over winter storms, tempests, and all the coldness, barrenness and emptiness. And the same light and power will go over the tempter's head, which power and light were before he was. And so in the light standing you will see your salvation, you will see the Lord's strength, you will feel the small rain, you will feel the fresh springs in the power and light, your minds being kept low, for that which is out of the power and light lifts up.[13]

Quakers seek to bring the whole of their lives into the silence, bringing the stresses of the world into the hovering, protecting, loving power of the Holy Spirit. We need, however, to be very careful to examine our promptings: perhaps they are only good ideas, the product of an over-engagement in mental activity because our minds are not 'kept low', submissive to the Spirit. Is the call that is experienced or heard in Meeting for Worship a call for human beings to work for humanitarian ideals, or for God to bring light into our darkness?

Concepts of ministry must of course be broad enough to include all the service Friends feel called to give to others, to the Society of Friends, to the world, but it must also be broad enough to include space for the response of the whole being to the love of God. It was said of Francis Hall, an American Quaker who was very active in trying to improve the social conditions of human kind, that he never lost touch with the inner Christ from which his social concern emanated. He emphasised the need for contemplatives: 'God is calling for a new host of contemplatives so that God may enter into them and flow through them and save the world' . . . Social action is right, but not if '. . . it becomes an appeal to human will without reference to the power of the Spirit (when) it misses the source and power of true religion.'[14]

PART II

IMAGES TOWARDS GOD

Brenda Clifft Heales

CHAPTER 3

The Transforming Image

Images can lead us to the source and power of the Holy Spirit, whether experienced by each of us individually, or collectively in our Meetings for Worship. How can images lead us, or open us towards God? In order to do this they first need to open us towards ourselves, so that we are in touch with our inmost being.

Images can be agents of transformation and healing for us. In images we experience eternal meaning shining through, or manifesting itself in, particular signs, symbols or metaphors. One of Jung's important discoveries was the way in which images and symbols are able to transform us. P.W. Martin has explored this discovery in relation to the religious life, and specifically to Quaker worship.

> Anyone wholeheartedly engaging in the experiment in depth will find, as a normal fact of experience, that the unconscious repeatedly produces shapes, objects, phrases, ideas, which have this peculiar quality: if put to their right use they make possible a re-direction of energy and, by so doing, progressively transform the man who uses them.

Later in the book he makes the following observation:

> When it is successful (which, needless to say, is not always) the Quaker Meeting for Worship is indubitably a method by which the deep centre is experienced and the experience transmitted . . . At its best, as in George Fox's day, the ministry has the character of the transforming symbol, bringing to the common fund words and images which make possible a new direction of energy.[1]

It is important for each of us to ask ourselves the question,

'What is my image, or what are my images, of God?' In our answers we will find that no single image alone suffices, but that we are able to relate to a wide range of images and that we find these helpful and meaningful depending on our mood and our particular circumstance. We will also find, on reflecting on our past lives, that there has been a succession of images as we have been affected by our physical and personal development and by our experiences. Our very early experiences may not seem to be religious or spiritual *per se*, but we need to examine very carefully those experiences in infancy and childhood which come to us in response to, or in connection with, the arts because here, in our imagination, are the first glimmerings of the 'inner teacher', the inner guide, the shaping Holy Spirit operating in our deepest being. It is for this reason that our experience of the arts is intimately connected with our experience of God.

It will, I hope, be helpful if I begin by describing some of my early experiences in relation to the operation of pictures and words upon my spirit.

One of my earliest memories of any kind is of my mother reading stories to me. One of the books she used when I was aged three or four is particularly vivid. It was called *Horton Hatches the Egg*.[2] As I heard the section of the story where Horton, who is an elephant, has to endure a bitterly cold winter sitting on a nest to protect a precious egg which has been abandoned by the feckless Maisie the Lazy Bird, and as I gazed at the picture of Horton with icicles hanging from his trunk, ears and tail, I entered into the experience. I think my mother was perturbed by my incoherent sobs about this cruel suffering, but something very important was happening. My compassion was called into being in an absolutely pure sense, because it was detached from any personal involvement which could have muddied it with feelings of guilt.

It was significant that this summoning of a deep part of myself came through both the pictures and the words which told the story in rhyme and rhythm (the story is written in verse). Both the visual and the verbal have continued to be important agents in my development. This ordering on the page of painful experience and the framing of the whole by the security of my mother's presence and the habitual pattern of the daily reading combined to make the experience safe.

When I was two or three years older, probably aged between five and six, another important experience occurred in a more specifically religious framework. At about this time someone gave me as a present the Book of Common Prayer. I was very baffled by this book which was quite unlike any other in my experience and I asked my mother what it was for. She said it was to use in church. I then asked what church was. Her exact words I do not recall, but her answer generally was that people went there to pray to God. Instantly I decided that if that was so, I must use this book for its proper purpose, although I do not think I had any notion of what prayer and God might be.

So I went to the Sunday School of St. Luke's, Clapham, the nearest Anglican church. Here I encountered images of God. The first intimation I had that God was a being was that she was Miss Armstrong, the Sunday School teacher. Calm, tall, graceful and poised, she must have had deep spiritual resources to make us feel so loved, and such children of God.

Other images manifested themselves in connection with some work which Miss Armstrong set us to do. We had to design and colour a border for a text. It was exciting and absorbing work, involving verbal and visual skills as I created colours and shapes which related to the text. I regret to say that I felt very scornful of the other children who made coarse scribblings round their borders with multi-coloured pencils. However my positive perception was that I was connecting line and colour and shape with religious meaning, and that rushing through just to get the task finished was no way to work. I recall deep, satisfying concentration as I laboured trying to do the task well, appropriately and with love. I felt connected in the deepest part of me to something other, calling out a response, insisting on attentiveness, and somehow finding form and expression.

I encountered another image of God when I was given in Sunday School a small, postcard-size, reproduction of Holman Hunt's *The Light of the World*. I remember the shock of recognition as I realised that Jesus was knocking on the door of our Sunday School. There he was with his lantern, standing on the rather dark pathway, overhung with trees, which connected the main church with the church hall where Sunday School was held. Although I found the picture of Jesus with his crown of thorns, long white gown and lantern, rather strange, I had no problem in recognising *where* he was. This sense of the immediacy of the surroundings and that there can be an experience of the divine in the little and the local was important, as was the sense of approaching something strange and unknown from a familiar and safe place.

As I grew into adolescence there were two streams which fed my spiritual growth. One was the Anglican church, and the other was my reading and response to the world of the imagination.

When I was nine we moved to Cliftonville, a suburb of Margate in Kent, so that my parents could live out a dream of having their own guest house. Although there were some attractions in living beside the sea, these were insufficient compensation for summers where my parents were overworked and spent their days constantly serving other people, or doing preparatory work for that service. Not only did I feel the loss of their attention, but I also had to help in various ways, doing jobs which on the whole I did not enjoy.

All I wanted to do was escape. I escaped into reading.

I read in all the interstices of time and space which became available; often I made them available in the most unlikely situations. I escaped to read in a corner of the kitchen, in the garden, the bedroom; I even locked myself into the bathroom. I was present not in the chaotic, busy world around me, but in the world which had been opened to me through books and my imagination.

There were many products of this intensive reading. It increased my knowledge of words and their meaning, and of places and times unknown to me. It also increased my insight into people, their motivation, feelings and experiences. It gave me vicarious experience of these other lives and so helped my deeper self to grow as I saw that of God within these images which peopled my imagination.

As I began to respond to poetry I began to feel something else happening. I had for some time responded to nature with intense emotion and this, combined with my religious sense gave me intimations of,

A presence that disturbs me with the joy
Of elevated thoughts; a sense sublime
Of something far more deeply interfused,
Whose dwelling is the light of setting suns,
And the round ocean and the living air,
And the blue sky, and in the mind of man.[3]

I felt I could participate in something of Wordsworth's experience as I gazed at beautiful scenes, or pictures or descriptions of such scenes. The poets I first liked were those who celebrated nature and who found in it an experience of the numinous.

I responded also to the sheer magic of words, the rhythm, the sound and the sense combining to move me into some strange place, into an awareness of something that was not the poem and not me, but both, and another mysterious presence. I didn't name it, quite, as an image of God, but I did recognise it as a religious experience.

Meanwhile, what had happened to my sense of Jesus as an image of God? He continued in one way to be the unreal figure in the gown in the Holman Hunt picture, contrasting with the dark, leafy intimacy of the rest of the picture, which gave the feeling of connectedness. The Anglican church I attended was middle-of-the-road, comfortable, consoling and not too demanding. Certainly I was uplifted by the power and beauty of the liturgy, if sometimes bored by its repetitiveness, and I often left services feeling charged with what I thought was religious feeling, but these vague, if glorious experiences did not seem to have a great deal of connection with my everyday self where life was sometimes rather hotly and desperately lived. The images of God experienced and proclaimed in worship had become detached from my deeper self.

Therefore, when I encountered the aggressive evangelism of one of the Billy Graham crusades to London I was quite unable to cope. Because I had not paid enough attention to my religious growth I was ambushed by Billy Graham's hell-fire certainties which invaded my very being. He was the first powerful religious leader I encountered. In the church there had been friendly Mr Powell, the Welsh curate, and kindly Mr Mellows, the vicar. But did they have spiritual power? Certainly Mr Mellows was kind, certainly he had insight. I still remember some of his sermons with absolute clarity. Certainly he never preached hell-fire and damnation, but was able to be both positive and humble as he pointed people towards God, and gentle and caring in his relationships with his parishioners. But he did not, was not able, to help me in a radical way when I had my Billy Graham crisis. He, in effect, patted me on the head and told me not to worry and that of course my father would not go to hell because he did not attend church. I needed more than warm reassurance, however. I needed to be able to use my mind, to be told which books would give informed and scholarly interpretations and insights which would be helpful.

My sense of betrayal was profound.
My images of God were destroyed.

I could not make the connection between my experience and the images of Jesus and of God which I heard proclaimed by Billy Graham with such certainty. They were for me not images towards God, but images away from God.

Painfully I began to face a world which was possibly God-less and I spent many years without any very definite belief in anything. The journey out of this wilderness to where I am now was long and complex and has been accompanied by considerable distress as well as great joy.

*   *   *

What are my images of God now?

They are, I think, to be found in the paradoxical images of stillness and of energy, and in a broken eggshell.

There are many traditional, poetic and artistic expressions of the paradox of God as stillness and energy. T.S. Eliot has called this, 'The still point of the turning world'.[4] It can also be seen in the experience of Moses who saw the bush burning with power and energy without being consumed. Moses has to stand and be.

And the angel of the Lord appeared to him in a flame of fire out of the midst of a bush; and he looked, and lo, the bush was burning with fire, yet it was not consumed.

And Moses said, 'I will turn aside and see this great sight, why the bush is not burnt.'

When the Lord saw that he turned aside to see, God called to him out of the bush, 'Moses, Moses!' And he said, 'Here am I.'

Then He said, 'Do not come near; put off your shoes from your feet, for the place on which you are standing is holy ground.'[5]

The place of burning energy has God in the centre, but the place of stillness, the place of the absolute concentration of Moses, is also holy ground, sacred space.

It is in the midst of the sounds of great earthquake and thunder that Elijah hears the still, small voice, the silence of God. The Pentecost experience was of invigorating, empowering energy in the images of tongues of fire and a rushing mighty wind, but the resurrection experience of two of the disciples on the road to Emmaus was the moment of silent recognition of a familiar action. The energy of George Fox is apparent in his Journal, but his image of the seed is that of contained energy, his image of light is that which makes us still, makes us submit and shows us that in this stasis power comes.

In art too the paradox of stillness and energy can be found. A painting is, in ordinary definition, a static artefact, but there is energy inherent in the cypresses, the cornfields, the starry skies in paintings by Van Gogh, there is the stillness of the captured contemplative moment in an interior by Vermeer and there is an aesthetic meditation in Cezanne's still life of apples on a wooden table. In painting and sculpture, line, shape and colour are creating an artefact which is in itself static and yet depicts both movement and stillness. The stillness is not, however, the deadness of the absence of movement, but is charged with energy. Keats expresses this paradox when he is describing the scenes depicted on the side of a Grecian urn:

Heard melodies are sweet, but those unheard
Are sweeter; therefore ye soft pipes play on;
Not to the sensual ear, but, more endeared,
Pipe to the spirit ditties of no tone.[6]

Or as Eliot says:

> Words move, music moves
> Only in time; but that which is only living
> Can only die. Words, after speech, reach
> Into the silence. Only by the form, the pattern
> Can words or music reach
> The stillness, as a Chinese jar still
> Moves perpetually in its stillness.[7]

Rembrandt's painting of Aristotle shows him standing with the bust of Homer and holding the Medallion of Alexander the Great. Here there is a complexity of visual images which refer us to Aristotle's ideas and Alexander's action in the world. This complexity is both honoured for its existence and ignored and dismissed in the deep, meditative contemplation of Aristotle in the picture which leads us towards the darkness and mystery and stillness of inner space.

These references to the Bible, to Fox's Journal, to art and literature are important in the connection they make between my personal God images and those I share from our inherited religious and aesthetic traditions. It is important that this connection is made, as it can be dangerous and delusive to cherish one's own images separately from the worshipping group whether they are one's contemporaries or one's ancestors.

Sometimes, however, one is given a personal image which seems to be powerful and highly individual. It is important not just to celebrate and proclaim such an image, but to reflect upon it, making connections both with one's own spiritual development and with other experiences and expressions of related images.

During the course of one of our *Appleseed*[8] weekends one small group had been given different concepts such as: hoping, depression, anger, searching, God. They had been asked to draw these concepts in a non-representational way, using shapes, lines and colours. As I worked with the group I found that I had drawn an image of God which was like half a broken eggshell. As I began to reflect upon it my first response was that it was an incomplete mandala. People often draw a mandala, or circle, as their image of God and I thought that mine was incomplete because my image of God was incomplete, showing that I needed to be listening more attentively in prayer and worship. I then reflected that it was incomplete also because no image of God can ever be complete. We have indeed only, 'hints and guesses, Hints followed by guesses.'[9]

My third reflection was that the image was not only related to the mandala of the circle but to the egg which is an archetypal image of new birth, of hope. I then perceived that the fractured sharp edges of the broken half were painful, but were also open, and were God's openness to us and also her woundedness and suffering alongside us. I also saw energy and stillness.

Neither the image I drew, nor the language I used to describe my response to the image, is complete and satisfactory to me as a representation of my experience of God. The image is nevertheless helpful to me because it points towards God; it is an approach to mystery.

*　　*　　*

An important recent experience has been the discovery of a new translation of St. John's Gospel which begins 'In the beginning was the Word, and the Word was toward God, and God was what the Word was.'[10]

Andy Gaus has translated all the Gospels from the original Greek. What he has done is to reveal the Gospels as if nearly two thousand years of history had not occurred. When I read this translation for the first time it was like the experience of seeing a picture, an 'old master', cleaned and restored. Layers of dirt and varnish are removed so that we see the picture in its freshness and lively colour. It has a kind of innocence and intimacy. Its brown glaze had seemed to be part of its respectable authenticity, part of its authority. Now its authority is seen not vested in the accumulated patina of years, not in a protective glaze which increases our sense of seeing through a glass darkly; instead authority is vested in the original perceptions of the experience. So it is with different translations of the Gospels.

In this translation I was brought to sudden, startled attention in the phrasing of the so-familiar opening words. One reads not, 'The Word was with God', but 'The Word was *toward* God'. This suggests not a static, achieved state, but a dynamic process, a yearning, a face turned towards the light, a relationship, a journeying. Language has a releasing power through its syntax, its choice of words, its paradoxes and its imagery. Today many people, and many Friends among them, are fearful and suspicious of language. How often do we hear the complaint that language is inadequate, and that words are limiting, separating and isolating.

The fear and suspicion are surely based on a lack of excitement about language together with the feeling that it must always be biddable, always a defining mechanism. But language is not like that unless it is a dead language. It is not mechanistic, but living and volatile. Words change their meanings over the centuries, even over the decades. The length and rhythm of sentences change and there are continuing subtle changes in word order and usage. T.S. Eliot complained about the problem of language:

Words strain,
Crack and sometimes break, under the burden,
Under the tension, slip, slide, perish,
Decay with imprecision, will not stay in place,
Will not stay still. Shrieking voices

Scolding, mocking, or merely chattering,
Always assail them.[11]

Throughout *Four Quartets* Eliot is stretching, pushing, urging language to express the inexpressible—our experience of the presence of God.

If a poet like Eliot has such problems with the volatility of language, we too might feel justified in feeling resentful of how it might distort our thoughts, how it interferes with meaning, how it will not, cannot, convey the experience we wish to communicate.

It is true that language does present us with difficulties. It is also true, however, that language is a major way in which we can communicate with ourselves and with each other. In the quotation from St. John's Gospel referred to above, the language in the translations previously available to us seems to have distorted the meaning. It has been suggested that this was perhaps because the Church felt it *had* to distort the meaning to combat various heresies. It is easier to have a definitive statement like, 'The Word was with God', even though that is in itself difficult and mysterious, than the strange dynamic process or relationship suggested by 'toward'. The more mysterious a meaning is, the more impossible it is to encapsulate it into neat and tidy credal statements. Friends have rightly always been suspicious and uneasy about these, seeing them as limitations of truth, as partial or distorted truth, rather than helpful descriptions. In credal statements, and in rigid, fundamentalist interpretations of the Bible, we can see the limiting power of language. But the language is limiting only because the people who used it wanted it to be limiting. Because they wanted power and authority—or even certainty—they needed closed statements, reductive, shrunken, prosaic definitions of the inexpressible, the glory, mystery and poetry of God.

There are many different uses of language, all legitimate, all necessary. Language, we are told, is a tool.

The practical use of words to order potatoes from the green-grocer or ask the way to the station is at one end of a spectrum of language use; at the other end is, 'The Word was toward God'.

The following are some of the important ways in which language is used:

— utilitarian; giving and getting information about one's practical and social needs.

— informative about inner needs; the attempt to describe to others one's inner experience, without which one would feel imprisoned in a solipsistic world.

— intellectual information about the nature of the world of science, geography, politics.

— persuasive language, slanted and subjective, seen in advertising and politics.

— imaginative language which is where language finds its creative self, where we create it anew and it creates us.

As Friends, open to new light, not bound in by the trapped language of creeds, or the structures of ritual and liturgy, we should be claiming the last category, imaginative language, as the language of Meeting for Worship. Not exclusively, of course; there is some place for the other kinds of language use. At the moment, sadly, it is the other kinds which are too often dominant when they reflect our pedestrian, earth-bound ministry.

Is it our language which is deficient or our experience? Hugh Valentine, in an article, suggests that part of our problem with religious language is a problem not with language but with God. 'It is as though there is a deep resistance within us to the very idea of encounter with God'.[12]

Is this true?

Do we try to encounter God? Or do we resist and take refuge in notions?

Do we try to describe, to share, our striving and our experience?

In a sonnet called *Prayer* the seventeenth century poet George Herbert struggles to find a way of using words to describe, to make real, what it is to pray.

Prayer the Church's banquet, Angel's age,
   God's breath in man returning to his birth,
   The soul in paraphrase, heart in pilgrimage,
The Christian plummet sounding heav'n and earth;
Engine against th'Almighty, sinner's tower,
   Reversed thunder, Christ-side-piercing spear,
   The six-days world transposing in an hour,
A kind of tune, which all things hear and fear;
  Softness, and peace, and joy, and love, and bliss,
   Exalted Manna, gladness of the best,
   Heaven in ordinary, man well drest,
The milky way, the bird of Paradise,
   Church-bells beyond the stars heard, the soul's blood
   The land of spices; something understood.[13]

Here we see a flowering of images, a piling up of metaphor upon metaphor, a reaching out from the actually known—church bells, the ordinary, a plummet—to the speculatively known—beyond the stars, Heaven—into mystery.

But it is not just in the dazzling inventiveness of the metaphors that Herbert, taking us with him, can approach God. It is in the struggle. The poem is a struggle, a series of different stepping stones, a succession of leaps into darkness and it is crowned by the deceptive simplicity of its final phrase, 'something understood'. This phrase is layered with resonant meaning, but only because of the struggle and the vivid imaginative power of the metaphors which precede it. It is layered and resonant *in context*.

The images are contained in a pattern, the pattern of rhythm and rhyme which are the discipline of the sonnet form. They do not arrive at a logical conclusion, nor do they reach an intellectual hypothesis; what they reach is the simplicity of 'something understood'. But this phrase is deceptively simple, because in it all the complexities, all the vivid imaginative power of the metaphors which precede it, meet each other in a point of stillness. 'Something understood' contains the struggle to understand *and* gives a glimmering of insight.

Surely this resembles the action of prayer itself. This is a major reason why the poem speaks so powerfully and is so helpful. Prayer is such a struggle to pay attention. It has various forms and modes, and at the heart of prayer is the moment of complete simplicity, the still small voice, the receiving of, never the whole truth, but, 'something understood'. This poem helps me to pray because it describes an experience and it is a prayer. Operating in some ways like a Zen koan[14] it comes through struggle into insight.

*   *   *

Metaphor and imagery are important ways of opening and extending our experience and of communicating with others. They are especially useful in describing our experience of God. For early Friends metaphor and imagery became major ways in which they described their experience of God and their understanding of the workings of the Holy Spirit. Friends found them helpful because they are neither manipulative nor restrictive in their expression and reference.

We are aware of much debate and discussion in the columns of *The Friend* and elsewhere about Christocentric or Universalist beliefs among British Friends. The controversy is especially sharply felt and hurts are most often experienced in relation to language which is perceived as contentious and therefore divisive.

Jesus's own language was not exactly bland.

He offered a wealth of metaphors, imagery and models of God for the imaginations of his hearers to work upon: the mustard seed, the sower, the candle, new wine into old skins, the true vine, the good shepherd, the leaven, the pearl of great price. The single truth he was pointing to in all this variety is that these are images, pictures, stories, which are towards God. We must use them to approach the mystery. Instead of definitions, limits and safety we have been given freedom and variety, growth and change and risk. Marion Milner, who has described how she has used the arts to lead her to deeper self-understanding and spiritual insight, makes a specific connection between what she found in the depths of herself and what she found in the Gospels:

> . . . when thinking about the kind of surrender of conscious planning experienced in making the drawings, phrases from the Gospels kept cropping up in my thoughts, such as . . . 'Consider the lilies of the field'. 'Take no thought for the morrow . . .' 'The meek shall inherit the earth.' In fact it almost seemed that on one level the symbolism of the Gospels was a kind of poetic handbook for the way in which psychic creativity works.[15]

Metaphor is 'toward God' because, far from being a picturesque way of saying something which could be said plainly in another way, it extends our experience. Metaphor makes available to us new meanings which can be expressed adequately in no other way, e.g.

'All things were new and all creation gave another smell unto me than before.' (George Fox).

'Know thy heart more and more ploughed up by the Lord'. (Isaac Penington).

'I am the Lord of the dance' (Sydney Carter).

Metaphor involves our emotions and our thoughts so that we are led into new significance, new understanding of the reality of our own experience of God, who is hidden, dark and other but also 'Closer is he than breathing, nearer than hands or feet.' (Tennyson).

When we minister in Meeting about our experience of God we are saying the unsayable—a task which can be seen as similar to knowing the unknowable. As Gregory of Nyssa says, 'Stammering, we echo the heights of God as best we can.'[16]

In their stammering the mystics have brought forth metaphors which often describe their human religious *experience*; they do not normally attempt to describe *God*.

As Janet Martin Soskice says:

It is . . . of the utmost importance to keep in mind the distinction, never remote in the writings of Anselm or Aquinas, between referring to God and defining Him. This is the fine edge at which negative theology and positive theology meet, for the apophatic insight that we say nothing of God, but only point towards Him, is the basis for the tentative and avowedly inadequate stammerings by which we attempt to speak of God and His acts. And, as we have argued, this separation of referring and defining is at the very heart of metaphorical speaking and is what makes it not only possible but necessary that in our stammering after a transcendent God we must speak, for the most part, metaphorically or not at all.[17]

We cannot define God either.

It is as true for us as for the mystics that we do not have to attempt such an awesome task. However, to describe our *experience* of God, or of the moving of the Holy Spirit within us, is important to mystics and Friends alike. Among Friends, as among other believers, the sharing of spiritual experience is central to the sense of belonging to a religious community, of 'being a people'.

When we are standing on the edges of our known experience and reaching out into the unknown, images can point us towards God.

* * *

Words, after speech, reach
Into the silence.

T.S. Eliot[18]

CHAPTER 4

Julian of Norwich:
A ministry of images

Julian of Norwich is a mediæval mystic who had a profound
experience of God. This experience was mediated to her through
a wealth of images. She spent many years reflecting on the revelations she had received that she understood their significance
for herself and so that they could be used to help others in their
search for God. She had important insights into the intimate
involvement of God in all suffering creation, a God who chooses
for a home the wasteland of our hearts. She offers a ministry of
images, and this chapter is an exploration of some of them.

Lionel Blue characterstically encapsulates the story of Julian
of Norwich in these words: 'You can come to God in many ways
. . . Julian of Norwich in the Middle Ages had a bad dose of 'flu,
ran a temperature and saw visions. She lived on them for the rest
of her life, and got herself walled up beside a Norwich church.
She was noted for her common sense.'[1]

Part of the humour derives from the highly selective nature of
this potted life story. Another part derives from its truth. One of
the reasons why Julian can speak to us today in the Society of
Friends is that she did see visions *and* she was noted for her
common sense, that she had a direct experience of God which
changed her life *and* she reflected on its meaning for herself and
her 'even Christians', i.e. all those who were on the same journey as she was. Her emphasis that she had experiences of God
'without any intermediary' was historically very significant
when she was writing; it should also endear her to Friends. So
perhaps it does not seem so strange that we should call for help
in healing our fractured ministry and in our search for metaphors

for transformation from a fourteenth-century recluse. The other important aspect of Lionel Blue's observation is not intended to relate to Julian specifically: 'You can come to God in many ways.' This, however, is one of the important insights which Julian is giving us, and she expresses this insight analytically and experientially.

The multifariousness of the 'Showings', the different ways in which they are experienced, the language used (with Christo-centric or universal mystical images, or with newly-minted parables) give us a broad awareness of many paths to God, many varieties of religious experience. All this rich, seeming disorder is contained within a framework of Julian's love of and con-fidence in God. Her faith gives her a safe structure in which to explore the complexities of her experiences. Before we look more closely at the text of her *Revelations*, we need to see Julian in context and to recognise that she was a mediæval person, influenced by the social, religious and intellectual life of her time.

Julian of Norwich was born towards the end of 1342. She tells us that the revelations were given in May, 1373, when she was thirty; she writes in Chapter fifty-one that she had been reflect-ing upon her visions for almost twenty years, so that part was written in 1393. She is named in wills as a beneficiary as late as 1416, so she was still alive then. She is therefore an almost exact contemporary of Chaucer.

We do not know whether she was already a solitary in 1373, at the time of the revelations. The wills and tradition certainly make it plain that eventually she was a recluse at Norwich, although we do not know if she ever became a nun. Her cell was supported by St. Julian's and St. Edward's church, Conisford, and this church belonged to the Benedictine community at Carrow.

In the fourteenth century the solitary life was almost popular in what was called the 'Golden Age of Recluses'. Hermits were male and sometimes itinerant, whereas an anchorite or anchoress would be enclosed in an anchorage. An anchoress or solitary might be theologically more sympathetic to Friends than a religious in a convent; we see in her an extreme form of individualism and refusal to conform, together with the need to affirm the direct, unmediated relation of the soul to God.

Many towns would have at least one solitary, and townspeople often contributed substantially to their upkeep in return for their ministry of prayer. Would-be recluses would have to make a formal claim that this was their calling, and such claims would be investigated by an officer of the church to check their spiritual authority and to ensure that the recluse would have adequate material means of sustenance. Once accepted, a recluse would then be walled into her anchorage with a spectacular and grim Mass, usually the Mass for the Dead. For Friends, who value their Meetings as loving communities and who find the sense of 'being a people' a source of great strength, this part of Julian's commitment may be found difficult, if not unacceptable. However few recluses endured utter physical solitude all the time and certainly Julian had at least two servants. Recluses' main activity was prayer, but some crafts were also practised. Recluses often acted as spiritual directors, advisers or counsellors, and we know that this is a ministry which Julian offered and for which she was much in demand.

Julian speaks to us in metaphor and imagery; indeed she received her understanding of God's nature through realistic, naturalistic visual images or visions, as well as through words in her mind. There is, in addition, a sense in which she herself is an image—a recluse, withdrawn from life, walled in from the outside world in order to pray and reflect., She can truly be said to inhabit sacred space. This is a reminder that at times isolation and separation from the ceaseless flow of daily life are a necessary condition for our spiritual journey. We can be fatigued and fretful as 'getting and spending we lay waste our powers'.[2] It does need great courage to make the journey as Julian did, alone. While in one sense this is true for all of us, as Quakers we can enjoy the paradox of being alone together.

Julian's ministry was not just for her age, but ours, and we in the Religious Society of Friends share, surprisingly, some common insights with her. In my own personal journey, Julian's insights have been an important part of my healing and my spiritual growth. There are several aspects of her ministry which seem to have especial relevance.

Firstly, it is exciting that Julian wrote in English. In choosing, like Chaucer, to write in her native tongue, she is one of those who celebrated it and aided its development into a flexible and expressive language for all to understand and use. Gradually the English language had been breaking free from the thrall of Latin and Norman French. In the fourteenth century important writers like Chaucer used English creatively in major works, pushing out the frontiers of its expressive power. She is also in the tradition of many of the women mystics in Europe who were writing in the vernacular. We can see Julian as part of these movements in her urgency to bring the good news of God's healing love directly in homely language to ordinary people, her fellow Christians. 'God longs to teach us to know him and love him for ever in a way which suits us and helps us.'[3]

She can also be linked with an important aspect of the convictions of seventeenth century Friends who were suspicious of the elitist, ornate, Latinate rhetoric which characterized the sermons preached in 'steeple houses' This rejection of learned, difficult language was part of the concept of the priesthood of all believers; it was not the elevated priests with their refined university rhetoric who were perceived as truly ministering, but those who, like the apostles, received a direct call—the unlearned, ploughmen, herdsmen and even women! It is important to understand, however, that the language of Julian and seventeenth century Friends alike was plain only in the sense of using the vernacular in simple, direct expression and construction; it was rich in vivid imagery, abounding in metaphors and Biblical references and quotations.

Secondly, as I read Julian's *Revelations* I experience a warmth and immediacy coming across the centuries. An important reason for this is that she is a woman writing with feminine insight. She is warm and personal and these qualities find expression in the easy flow of her language. This is partly because the style of the *Revelations* is closer to the spoken than to the written word. Possibly she dictated her *Revelations* to a scribe; certainly she seems to speak directly to me. She is part of my journey which began with Miss Armstrong in the Clapham Sunday School. I have a strong need to experience the feminine in my images of God and to see God operating in and through women who are spiritually empowered. Julian herself searches for God our Mother and her imagery in describing our relationship with God and Jesus is sometimes uncompromisingly feminine, and sometimes challenging in her abrupt linking of contrasting images: God is our Father, our Mother, our true Lord.

Thirdly, she makes us feel safe because her certainty and her affirmation that 'all shall be well' are based on a deep experience of the dark places and coming through them. She has no glib reassurances. One of her most compelling qualities is her honesty. We trust her because she constantly questions the meaning of her experience and admits her bafflement when faced with conflicting aspects of God's love and God's truth. The famous affirmations which are often quoted, 'All shall be well' and 'I am the ground of your being,' are too often seen out of context and are then delusively facile and simplistic.

What these sayings actually relate to is the conflict which Julian experiences between the Church's teaching on punishment, hell and damnation and the truth of her own vision that God loves us. She cannot understand how all can be well if some are to be eternally damned. She cannot reconcile the Church's teaching that sinners deserve blame and wrath with the fact that she can see no blame or wrath in God. The answers she receives include both the direct words she hears in the vision that, 'All shall be well,' and 'What is impossible to you is not impossible to me,' and the new parable she is given of the Lord and the Servant.

All of this spoke directly to my condition after my earlier damaging experience of fundamentalist certainties. Here was someone with everything to lose, because she could have been accused of heresy, and burned at the stake, simply for making a courageous, open searching of her truth and the Church's truth. Here was a deeply centred mystic who affirmed God's love and saw God's code of justice as descriptive, not prescriptive. 'Sin is more painful than hell . . . because sin is diametrically opposed to our essential nature.'[4]

In her lengthy reflection on sin, Julian offers her description of what she has been led to understand is its nature. 'It is all that is not good, the despicable shame and utter self-emptying Christ endured for us in his life and his dying, and all the physical and spiritual suffering and pain of the whole of creation. Sin itself has no substance—it is only known through the pain it causes.'[5] Here I found the connection between spirituality and psychology, here were restored an image of God and an image of Jesus, lost in adolescence and now reclaimed.

It will be seen that it was specifically personal issues which led me to find in Julian a mystic and a writer who is able to nurture me. There are also connections between her teaching and experience and that of the Society of Friends and I have tried to indicate some of these. We now need to examine more closely some of the images she received in her revelations.

These images were healing, opening and growing points for Julian, they have been for me, and I think they can be for other Friends also. They are an important part of our Christian mystical inheritance. They have a further importance in that they show the process of the transforming power of images, a process which needs to be part of our personal growth and which also needs to be operating in our Meetings for Worship.

There are sixteen revelations and Julian tells us that fifteen of these followed each other beautifully and smoothly during the course of one night. The sixteenth revelation happened the following night and concluded and confirmed the other fifteen. Part of the *Revelations* describes the immediacy of these visions and part shows Julian reflecting, analysing, questioning, as she continues to develop her understanding of them.

Seven of the revelations derive from the crucifixion and are in response to Julian's wish to see and understand Christ's suffering and the suffering of those around the cross. She wants to *share* it, to experience the anguish of dying, 'because I wanted to be fully purged by the mercy of God and afterwards live a life more in the true worship of God.'[6]

So the first image is that of the cross and the suffering figure of Jesus upon it. The cross is not an easy or accessible image for many twentieth-century Quakers in Britain and Julian's descriptions do not make it any easier for us. I think, however, that she has some important teaching for us about the nature of God's involvement in suffering.

The descriptions of Christ's passion can be very difficult for a modern reader although we are indeed familiar with television's close focus on suffering and dying in so many news bulletins. In Julian's words, 'The loss of blood and the terrible pain within his body and the harsh wind and cold outside all combined . . . and, as time went on, gradually dried up Christ's flesh . . . in this way I saw the sweet flesh wither bit by bit with dreadful suffering.'[7]

This is a vision of bleak suffering, taken to the extremes of what Julian can contemplate, so much so that it becomes her own suffering. She takes the passion of Christ into herself and could not, she says, imagine greater suffering if she herself were experiencing it because, 'Of all the pains that lead to salvation this is the worst; to see the one you love suffer.'[8]

I think there is a further connection between Julian's empathy with Jesus's intense agony and our experience of suffering. Firstly Julian is tempted to look away from the suffering body on the cross to heaven, but she resists the temptation. 'I did not want to look up. I would rather have remained in that pain and suffering until the end of the world than come to heaven in any other way than through him.'[9] She *has* to stay with the pain and suffering and when she does:

> I tried with all my concentration to see the moment of his death and expected to see his utterly lifeless body, but I did not. Just when I thought that his life could last no longer and that his death was bound to be revealed to me, suddenly as I looked at that same cross the expression on his face changed to joy. This made me change too, and I was as glad and joyful as could be . . . I was to understand that he means us to know that when we remain on that same cross with him in our pain and suffering, to the point of death, and with his help and grace holding on to the very end, then suddenly we shall experience his change of expression and we shall be with him in heaven. Without a moment's pause we shall pass from one state to the other and we shall all be brought into joy.[10]

What is Julian saying here? This is a very important insight as she reflects on her temptation to look away from the suffering to heaven. This is surely the temptation to rely on 'nice experiences' and consoling escapism as a path to healing and to God. In fact such 'pretty place' meditations can be a dangerous and delusive path away from God. We need to own our suffering, to look at it and not try to pretend it is not there. In such pretence we shall then miss finding God who is in the suffering with us and for Julian this is explicitly seen in the figure of Jesus on the cross who accepted the pain and endured 'to the very end'.

The experience Julian described can be compared with that of Peter Wood, who is a Friend from Hebden Bridge Meeting.

Peter Wood has described the great suffering he experienced when his partner, Neil, died of AIDS-related diseases. The relationship began with an awareness of deep mutual love and caring and much happiness was found, even after the discovery that Neil was HIV positive:

> Much of our time during this period was spent walking and camping, particularly in the fells and moors and mountains. These were often precious times during which we had a great sense of being at one with our surroundings. We experienced a stillness so vivid and intense that it was as though nothing else existed but during which we knew that all was right with the world and we had an overwhelming sense of our place in creation. These became known as our 'times with God' and were to awaken my spiritual quest, a journey I'd left firmly behind when I left the Church of England at the age of fifteen.

> The progression of AIDS caused Neil to have long periods of total exhaustion and severe night sweats, and made him susceptible to many opportunistic infections. As Neil's health deteriorated, I was often overwhelmed by anger and despair and yet whenever I needed to be there for him, to hold him during the long evenings by the fire, sometimes in silence, sometimes listening to music, reading or sharing a crossword

puzzle, it was as though I too, was being held, not only by Neil, but by God. It seemed that God was carrying my anger and despair to enable me to be there in the moment with Neil.

During the last six months of Neil's life his condition rapidly deteriorated, and I was to become aware that I was often dealing with my needs through him, and that if I was to be fully there for him, I had to put my needs to one side and fully support his decisions.'

Peter continues to describe the progression of Neil's illness and his own feelings in the ensuing months until it became clear that Neil's life was no longer tenable as the things that sustained him were out of his reach. Peter goes on:

He took the decision to withdraw from all treatment apart from pain control, knowing clearly what this would ultimately mean. Once again I had to put aside my needs, particularly my need for him to live, and respond to what was going on inside me, at my spiritual centre, allowing myself to grieve as well as supporting Neil's decision-making and showing my love for him in an unconditional way by starting the process of letting go.

The last week of his life Neil was in a semi-coma, and as I washed him on the final Sunday morning he started to take his last breaths. I held his hand and was able to experience his death as a very natural ending. Being there for him opened up a startling beauty of the moment, an experience I'd least expected.

Here we see the truth of the need to own and know our pain experienced by a fourteenth-century recluse and a twentieth-century gay man. It is expressed by the one in 'God language' and essentially Christocentrically, and by the other in language which is human, humane but also God-centred. It is a truth with resonance in theology, psychology and spirituality. In theology, the concept of a God who is self-giving, who suffers and who partakes of our humanity, is central; in psychology we understand the need to enter into and own our experiences whether good or bad, to *have* our experiences, not bury them or marginalise them, so that unhealed wounds fester. In our spiritual lives we find God in our deepest experiences at the centre of our being. It is also only from this depth that true ministry, in or out of Meeting, arises.

Julian's vision of the crucifixion is universal as well as essentially personal. It is a central image in her *Revelations* upon which she reflects and meditates. It is, however, not only the depth but also the breadth of Julian's images of God which can sustain us. The language she uses to describe the reality of the crucifixion is vividly naturalistic, drawing details from local scenes for its figurative power. Her vocabulary is local, not in its references to first century Palestine, but fourteenth century Norwich. For example, in her description of Jesus's blood flowing she compares it to 'great drops . . . like pellets' and 'drops of water off the eaves of a roof after a heavy shower of rain, tumbling so thickly that no-one could count them' . . . 'And as they (the drops of blood) spread out on the forehead they were as round as the scales of a herring.'[11]

These similes are local, almost shockingly commonplace, yet reassuring. She repeats them, sums them up. They are meant. They make the connection in our imagination between God most high and incomprehensible and God who is suffering on the cross in local, human circumstances. They are images taken from daily life and contain the reassurance of ordinary living. They connect terrible suffering in far-off Palestine with everyday Norwich. They connect us with God. This for Julian is the meaning not only of the crucifixion but the incarnation. God is both inner and local, and out there beyond our comprehension.

57

These startling images of Christ's blood seen in terms of 'herring scales' and 'pellets of rain from the eaves of a roof' are reaching out to express the inexpressible. 'Heaven in ordinary' as Herbert said in his poem.

Other images also derive from the experience of day-to-day living. Not all of life involves living on the verge of our ability to cope and Julian's awareness of God as comforter and protector in more ordinary times is seen in the homely, physical image of clothing, used to convey God's intimate closeness.

> As the body is clad in clothing, and the flesh in the skin, as the bones are in the flesh and the heart in the chest so are we soul and body clothed in and enfolded in the goodness of God— yes and more closely, for while all these physical things may waste away and wear out, God's goodness is always whole, nearer to us than anything else.[12]

The image of clothing is familiar, warm, domestic, consoling, close and intimate. Our clothes protect us from the extremes of heat and cold, from accidental hurts, from dirt. They become part of us, acquire our shape as they wear with our lives. This is an image of a God close and humble beyond our imagination or our hope.

Another domestic image Julian uses, and one which connects also with our creativity, is knitting. In Chapter fifty-seven she describes the unity of our soul and body in God:

> For our kind which is the heyer part is knitt to God in the makyng; and God is knitt to our kinde which is the lower part in our flesh taking; and thus in Christ our ii kinds are onyd (Middle English Text).[13]

Once again Julian uses the intimate and the familiar to point towards truths which seem beyond our comprehension.

In Chapter ten, the image of the sea bed is used:

Once my understanding was led down into the sea bed, and there I saw hills and green dales, which seemed to be covered with moss, and also seaweed and gravel. Then I understood the following: that if a man or a woman were under the wide waters, if he or she saw God there, as God is with people continually, he or she would be saved in body and soul and suffer no harm, and more than this, she would have more solace and comfort than can be imagined; for it is God's will that our experience is believing that we see him continually.[14]

This is a similar experience to that expressed in Psalm 139 and the theme is also similar: that it is impossible to be beyond the reach of God. The image of the sea is here used by Julian to express a condition of remoteness, of being out of our normal element and removed from normal experience. She sees God as present when we hardly know how to be present to ourselves in an alien environment which she also shows to be beautiful and realistic. This naturalistic image can be seen to contain both the ocean of light and the ocean of dark. It is also perhaps connected with the need to let go.

Another image is also about the importance of letting go. In one of her most famous visions of 'a tiny thing, the size of a hazelnut' she is given to understand that God made it, God loves it and God looks after it 'and so all things have their being through the love of God.' She stresses, however, that what matters is not her love for the hazelnut, or any other created thing, but her love for God.

We need to know the smallness of created things and to see no value and importance in what is created in order to love and know God who is unmade. This is the reason why our hearts and souls are ill at ease, because we seek rest in small things in which there is no rest, and do not know our God who is total might, wisdom and goodness; in him is true rest.[15]

Here Julian uses the simple, but potent symbol of the hazelnut to express a difficult paradox in theology. The creation is good and loved by God; the creation alone, however, will leave us dissatisfied and full of empty yearning. We have to let go of our desire to possess it because that stands in the way of openness to God.

Julian's imagery describing our relationship with God is sometimes uncompromisingly feminine. God is our Father, our Mother, our true Lord. In startling, perhaps uncomfortable imagery she describes Jesus as our true Mother who went into labour for the full time, suffering birth pangs to give birth to our eternal happiness. She compares a mother suckling her child with Jesus feeding us the holy sacraments.

In a possibly more acceptable image for Friends, Jesus is compared with a good mother who knows the needs of her child and looks after him with tenderness. She allows her growing child to be punished to break him of faults and teach him to develop virtues and graces. In this way Jesus is a natural mother to us. Whether or not you are comfortable with this imagery, it is important to see the feminine aspect of God. Christianity has been criticised, and not only by feminists, for its lack of inclusion of the feminine principle. Julian can truly be seen as a woman of our time in her vision of God as male and female, yin and yang, god and goddess.

Julian uses the images of being grounded and rooted in relation to several experiences. 'I am the ground of your beseeching,' comes from the three chapters on prayer. Prayer, she says, unites the soul to God and this is how she uses the image of 'I am the ground.' God is the ground, bedrock, base, earth, support, foundation—all these images are contained within the image of ground, that which comes from below to support us, nourish us, stabilise us. God is there already, Julian says, 'He wants us to know the truth about reality, which is that he is Being itself.'[16] This is an expression of the concept of God as our essential self. Julian's understanding of what knowing God is sounds astonishingly modern; it is the same as truly, deeply knowing ourselves. In Jungian terms, if we live only in our ego, or consciousness, creating a persona and projecting all our problems outwards, then we cannot know what our real self is. We must really get to know our own true self, our soul, because until we have done so we can never really know God. Until the soul reaches its full maturity we cannot be completely holy, or whole. They are the same. Julian's equating of the finding of God with our own wholeness is now becoming more generally accepted as a definition of the religious way.

God is nearer to us than our own soul, for he is the ground in which our soul stands, and he contains and holds our essential being and our physical nature so that they shall never separate. Our soul sits in God in true rest, and stands in God in true strength; it is rooted, because of its very nature, in endless love.[17]

These are just some of the images Julian experiences and explores in her *Revelations*. As with all imagery, they have power in so far as we feel them upon our pulses and apprehend their significance. For Julian both the revelations themselves and the insights given by years of reflection upon them are part of a ministry of love. Her last chapters are a vision of life, love and light and the certainty that, 'Love was what our Lord meant' when he gave the visions.

Do you want to know what our Lord meant in all this? Understand this utterly. Love was his meaning. Love was what he meant. Who showed it to you? Love. What did he show you? Love. Why did he show it? Because of love. Hold this to yourself and you shall understand and know more about love but you shall never know anything else from it.
So I was taught that love was what our Lord meant.[18]

PART III

FRIENDS AND SILENCE

Chris Cook

On one side of the mountain a path winds upwards through varying kinds of scenery. Some of that scenery one might want to spend time enjoying; other kinds might be less absorbing. There are places to stop and gaze, places for rest and refreshment, places of challenging steepness. There are birds and animals, fruit and flowers, streams and stagnant pools. There are briars, bogs, fallen trees, wasps and mosquitoes. There will be moments of breathtaking beauty, as well as terror of the chasm that opens suddenly before you. It is rarely dull.

On the other side of the mountain, the slopes are bare—nothing but scree and bare rock. There is a path, but it is difficult to distinguish from the mountain face. There might be a view, but it is completely hidden by dense mist. Yet this is the self-same mountain, the self-same summit.

Part III of this book is concerned mainly with the bare mountain, or—to use another image—the bare God.

It is my argument, and my experience, that the obverse of images is imagelessness, that God has an aspect for which we cannot possibly dream up useful images, and that this aspect of God can best be described as absolute silence. I believe this has implications for the way in which spiritual growth can be nurtured, for what Friends do in Meeting for Worship, and for how Friends might view (and practise) ministry in the world.

My companions and supports in trying to explore the meaning and implications of the Elijah-experience (the sound of God's silence) have been a sixth century monk and a thirteenth century friar, and I will be sharing in Part III some of their insights. I have come to respect and even love these two who travelled so much further up the bare mountain than I, and I hope some of this feeling will emerge through the technicalities and complications of trying to talk about absolute silence and find explanatory images for that which cannot be imagined.

CHAPTER 5

The Secret Silence

The phrase that heads this chapter comes not from an early Friend, but a sixth century Syrian monk. Known as Dionysius the Areopagite, or pseudo-Dionysius, he wrote a number of works which tried to bring together the philosophy of Plotinus (himself influenced by Plato) and the Christianity of his own day, much as modern theologians seek to make Christianity 'relevant'. The attraction of Plotinus's teaching lay in his attempts to explain how it could be that although God was obviously indivisibly One, the creation (the world we experience) was equally obviously 'many', even divided against itself. He also wanted to explain how it was that we, who are created beings and thus part of the world of 'many-ness', could still have ideas about the One, and even seek experience of it. That is rather like water seeking to become oil.

From the second century AD onwards the church paid a lot of attention to the right vocabulary for describing that aspect of God which allowed many to become One. This paradox is at the heart of traditional Christianity, which claims that God is One, yet also Three.[1] On the whole, arguments about the Trinity have not held Friends' attention or interest, mainly because we associate all that with creeds and notions. We are content to rest gently on the edges of one heresy or another, and give our attention to less notional (and confusing) matters like prison reform or Oxfam. But for early Christians this was a burning issue, because it conditioned their view of the world and (more important) their role in the world. They achieved a sort of working model of how this coming into unity with the One might happen, by paying attention to the relations between God and Jesus.

65

They believed that in Jesus divine nature and human nature became one, a unity, so Jesus was a meeting point between the human race and God. There were various theological words for this, such as atonement, redemption, reconciliation, or salvation, but all, basically, say the same: that the coming together of God and human nature in Jesus bridged the previously unbridgeable divide between the One (God) and the many (us and the rest of creation).

Dionysius in the sixth century inherited that working model and the traditional language describing it, but found it somehow inadequate, unrelated to his experience of God. The key word in Dionysius's writing is 'silence'. He claims to have experienced God as silence; and he says that the route towards that experience is helped or otherwise by the language people use about God. This idea becomes clearer when one looks at the four categories of language that distort views of God.

1. The first category is quite small, and consists of descriptions of God that would not fit in any circumstances—for example, that God is silly, or ignorant.

2. The second category is something of a grey area: those words about God which may be acceptable at some times or by some people, but not at others or elsewhere. Here most of us now know that we have to be careful, either because such words are not necessarily true in every time or culture, or because they might give offence to others. Such words might be that God is 'angry', or 'jealous'; or that God is a father (or mother).

3. Third, there are words normally regarded as 'praise' words, such as that God is 'kind', 'loving', 'caring', etc. It is less obvious that caution needs to be exercised in using these words, because they are the bedrock of most thinking about God. But the truth is that even these normally acceptable words are incomplete descriptions of God, or even, sometimes, positively misleading. Ideas of love, for example, are conditioned by lim-

[handwritten margin note: Is 'silence' itself an image/or a symbol of of God – how restrictive is it as such ....
God freed from all/ever images may manifest in whatever .....way not thinkg image]

ited circumstances: and thinking people have become very aware, in the late twentieth century, of the limitations and difficulties of describing God as a loving parent, let alone a father. And does one mean by 'love' what the pop song means?

4. Fourth: even the very best (largest and most beautiful?) image of God can mislead us, when we become attached to the image or metaphor or model, and mistake it for the reality it is supposed to represent. Friends are vocal about the wrongness of attachment to (or even worshipping) the kind of images one might find in some churches, and in that they are true heirs of the Reformation: but are they clear of attachment to the image of the Inner Light? That is an image of God, a kind of stepping-stone to absolute-God: and anyone who stands still too long on a stepping-stone is liable to fall into the water.

Dionysius takes all this a stage further. He says that it is misleading to be seeking any image of God, because no image whatsoever can do more than speak a partial truth. This is quite simply because all images are drawn from the very world of 'many-ness' the worshipper is seeking to get beyond. Thus, only when all images have been abandoned (visual, verbal, philosophical, theological, or whatever) can any of us reach what we really want and what God really is. — *[handwritten: ... truth God may have expressed, spoken ..]*

*   *   *

The practice of denying God any images or descriptions is known as the 'apophatic' tradition, from *apophasis* (Greek), meaning 'denial'. It does not mean denying oneself, either in the sense of giving up marmalade for Lent or of sacrificing oneself for others. What is being denied, or given up, is images, models and notions of God.

This is difficult to get one's mind around. Yet a look at personal experience, spiritual journeys, suggests that Dionysius's method is at work even when it is not being used consciously.

People do in fact shed images of God as they grow in their spiritual lives (and there is something very wrong if they do not). What satisfied them as children drops away (or is transformed into something new) as their religious experience grows. This is not to say that the old images were wrong; only that they no longer fit more adult experience. And what Dionysius is urging is simply a conscious, deliberate effort to intensify what should already be happening.

The God experienced at the end of this process Dionysius addresses thus:

> Higher than any being, any divinity, any goodness!
> Guide of Christians in the wisdom of heaven!
> Lead us up beyond unknowing and light,
>> up to the farthest, highest peak
>>> of mystic scripture,
>>>> where the mysteries of God's word
>>>>> lie simple, absolute and unchangeable
>>>>>> in the brilliant darkness of a hidden silence.[2]

Of course, Dionysius actually does use images to convey his experience of God. But they are paradoxical, almost self-contradictory images that seem to have little logical meaning. It is a problem of this tradition and this kind of experience of God that one has to use images to speak of that which is imageless. Would it be better to remain silent?

Some thought so. Dionysius had considerable influence on the Orthodox Christian tradition, producing the theology of hesychasm. Hesychasm developed, over many years, the deliberate denial of attributes of God through the cultivation of 'inner silence'. This is different from outer silence. Friends do not have to sit very long in a Meeting for Worship before realising that although we are outwardly silent, plenty of inner chatter is going on: and even when day-to-day thoughts die away, we sometimes

68

find ourselves describing (often with a view to spoken ministry) of.
rather than actually experiencing God.

The tradition of inner silence is less evident in the history of western Christianity, though it appears as contemplative prayer among the enclosed monastic orders, and in all monastic traditions there is an element of silence. It is then perhaps rather surprising that close attention to silence should appear in a radical Protestant movement such as early Quakerism.

I am not, of course, saying that the apophatic tradition was well known to George Fox and his contemporaries (though it could certainly be said that they were apophatic about the church, if not about God!). But early Friends had a powerful sense that something happened in the silence of Meeting for Worship which did not happen in the liturgy of other churches; and this certainly echoes what Dionysius had said a thousand years earlier about the God beyond words and images.

How did the tradition pass from Dionysius to seventeenth century Europe?

*   *   *

The answer seems to be that it came via Meister Eckhart, a German Dominican friar (1260–1327). Eckhart became an influential administrator and preacher for the Dominican Order, which had been founded in 1215. He travelled widely in Europe as an overseer of Dominican convents, teaching in Cologne and Strasburg at the Dominican 'schools' (proto-universities), and preaching to ordinary congregations. This was a period when so many were joining the monastic orders that it was impractical to teach them all Latin, which had hitherto been the academic, theological, diplomatic and cultural language of Europe. A new phenomenon for Meister Eckhart and his contemporaries was the need to express difficult and complex ideas (for which Latin was well-suited) in his native German. He had, as it turned out, a genius for this. When he uses German his teaching is alive with the sense of frontiers being pushed out, of limits being stretched to squeaking point. The same process is seen at work a hundred years later in Julian of Norwich, and two hundred years later in Martin Luther.

Pushing theology, via everyday language, to the limits of its capabilities brought Eckhart into conflict with the central authority of the church. It was a kind of pre-run of what happened to Martin Luther during the Reformation. Eckhart denied heresy, hotly, though he admitted mistakes: but in the end, shortly after he died, he was officially declared a heretic.

The net result of this was to deny Europe his writing for six hundred years: but his teaching did not disappear. His students and his hearers (monastic and secular) noted down his sermons and lectures virtually verbatim and these notes survived, alongside his secretly preserved books and tracts, in the monastic libraries of Europe, awaiting the nineteenth century revival in Germany of interest in his work.

Meanwhile, however, his influence was keenly felt in the European tradition through the teaching of his 'disciples' who—learning the lesson of his condemnation as a heretic— preserved his teaching in a modified form. The school of Rhineland mystics, Tauler and Suso in particular, owed much of their theology to Eckhart, and they passed it on to Ruysbroeck, Luther and Boehme (and even, eventually, to the Spanish mystics John of the Cross and Teresa of Avila, though they are outside the tradition I am describing).

From the Rhineland mystics Eckhart's thought passes into the common bloodstream of European religious thought and language.

Eckhart's 'masters', in terms of theology, were Dionysius and St. Augustine, mediated to him by Thomas Aquinas and Albertus Magnus (also members of his order). He draws, therefore, not only on the scholastic theology of his day with all its Latin neatness, but also upon the much less tidy Orthodox tradition of Dionysius. There are few new ideas—but then there are few new ideas in the Gospels. But of paramount importance—and how dear this should make him to Friends—was his own religious experience.

What is new in Eckhart's teaching (as in that of Jesus or George Fox) is the way in which traditions are brought together with personal experience of God, and the resulting insights expressed. It does amount to a new vision of the nature of God and the implications of it for humanity. And because there is a new vision, there is a new mode of expression, conveying both the information and the excitement. This has to do with the birth in Eckhart's time of German as a language in which serious theology could be expressed. Similar changes are happening in late twentieth century Europe with the coming together not only of some of the different Christian traditions, but also the tentative and patchy rapprochement of the world faiths. For all of us, as for Eckhart, this is an exciting and risky time, which requires new language.

The new use of German to express complex theology set Eckhart free to juxtapose apparently contradictory images, and thus by the very language he used convey the truth that at the heart of God there is a paradox. He does not so much tell, as show this as a fact of his own experience. He shares with the reader the actual experience of living inside a paradox. Cyprian Smith calls his account of Eckhart's teaching and its relevance to us today *The Way of Paradox:* early in the book he speaks of Eckhart's special way of thinking and of using language.

It is this which enables him not merely to *talk* about spiritual realities, but at the same time to kindle in his listeners an awareness that these realities truly exist, that we have only to

71

reach out in order to be able to touch them. Things which previously we had only heard or read about, now begin actually to impinge on our consciousness, and the spiritual quest emerges as something possible and eminently desirable.[3]

What Eckhart says is this.[4]

It is a commonplace of mediæval theology that there are two aspects of God, or two paradoxical truths. There is the aspect which can be known because God presents a kind of self-image in ways normal human faculties can grasp (however dimly!). One name for this is revelation. God has made her/himself available to our understanding in three modes, faces or persons: we can grasp these with intellect and with feelings. Some people find the fatherly/motherly/creatorly activity of God speaks to their condition. Others relate well to God personified in Jesus, either as an historical person or as a continuing word (or communication) from God, or both. Others can most happily live with the idea of the unbodied presence and activity of God, which some call the Holy Spirit. Most Friends would probably be happy in this last group, provided we were near the door marked EXIT.

However, this trinitarian 'aspect' is not the whole truth about God. There is another aspect of God, for which one might use the phrase 'God's inner being'. This aspect of God cannot be experienced in the world simply because God does not present it there. Therefore it cannot be grasped by faculties whose function is to process information from the world, faculties that feed on sense-perception.

Further: even when the inner being of God *is* experienced, it cannot be described. This is not because one is overwhelmed, dismayed, frightened or speechless in the ordinary sense (although one would be that too), but rather because all language, all imagery, all models and constructs and (therefore) ideas, are drawn from the world via sense-perception, directly or indirectly, and are inseparable from time and logic. Abolish time, and you abolish logic; abolish logic, and you abolish language, models, plans, ideas and constructs. Equally, if you abolish the sense-world, you abolish all that we mean by feelings. I am not, of course, speaking of temporary sense-deprivation, which produces the entirely real feeling of fear; but of a situation in which there never had been, were not, and never would be any sense perceptions. All of us feel fear at that thought; but we could not feel fear if we were actually in that situation.

Eckhart is saying, then, that God's inner being is permanently and absolutely out of reach of world-orientated faculties, because it 'contains' nothing remotely like the things known in a normal human way. When in everyday life one suddenly sees a shape one cannot identify, one is not able to make any sense of it. One is unable to grasp what it is until one can find something like it in one's past experience, a pigeon-hole in which to put it. This experience is wonderfully described in a passage in A.A. Milne's *Winnie-the-Pooh*. Piglet has gazed down into a Heffalump trap, not knowing what to expect, and has been roared at by the Heffalump he had hoped not to find. He flees to the safety of Christopher Robin, uttering inarticulate cries, unable to put any name to the horror he has seen. Language collapses under the strain. However, in the calming presence of Christopher Robin, he begins to search through previous experience for some way of conveying what he has experienced. Asked what it looked like, he replies:

> Like—like—It had the biggest head you ever saw, Christopher Robin. A great enormous thing, like—like nothing. A huge big—well, like a—I don't know—like an enormous big nothing. Like a jar.[5]

Well, of course, it *is* a jar, stuck on the head of his friend Winnie-the-Pooh. The readers know that. But Piglet does not.

This very funny tale contains a serious truth about the way in which we experience the unknown and try to understand it. If it is impossible to grasp the unknown until we have connected it with something known, it must be impossible to grasp at all what is by its very nature unconnected with anything else we know.

But if this aspect of God, God's inner being, is unknowable by our normal faculties, and indescribable, what am I doing trying to speak of it? Eckhart asked the same question; and it was Dionysius who supplied the answer. The inner being of God is, by definition, everything that the world is not, and the world includes God as revealed in it. This takes us straight back to the apophatic tradition, the via negativa, the saying-what-God-is-not. Eckhart uses this means with rare skill and humour, trying to break through stultifying thought-structures with statements about what God is not. 'Moral?' he said in a sermon. 'Moral, God is not. I am more moral than God!' What does he mean? That 'moral' is a human term, so it follows that the inner being of God is *not* like that.

Nor is it like anything else we can imagine or formulate; and this is precisely what the apophatic tradition tries to cope with. It accepts that there are any number of characteristics of which we can say 'the true nature of God is not that.' But the apophatic tradition also says that there is one ultimate apophasis, one apophatic statement that somehow sums up all the others. It is this: God's inner being cannot be *multiple* in any way whatever—not Trinity with divided functions; not creator/created/spirit.

I could put this another way, along with Eckhart. Inside that inner being God is utterly, permanently and indivisibly one: still, at rest, not going forth or returning home to itself. Eckhart speaks of the inner being of God as a desert, emptiness, nothing-at-all, silence.

Please pause at this point, and take full hold of what is being said: that what is 'really' at the centre of God is absolute silence.

· anotin iclea/refer of 'that of God'

· Apprehending the Energy...

No words are in there, no images, nothing at all: absolute silence.

This, ultimately, is why we cannot know or experience the inner being of God via faculties bound by things in the world and the ideas that spring from those things: there is simply nothing, no-thing, there to grasp. Our information-related intellect and emotions cannot see anything to get hold of; and as we have seen, they can only understand the unknown when it can be related to something already known, however distantly—like Piglet and the jar.

I have made a great issue of this absolute inner silence of God, because I believe that it is the matrix of true silence in Meeting for Worship and in the world. All human beings are at heart seeking for it, drawn towards it. It is our destination, and we have a special faculty that enables us to respond to its call. This is the faculty by which we 'know' God without the intermediary of intellect, senses, or emotions: we can experience God, as Eckhart puts it, *ohne mittel*, with no go-between. That seems to me highly significant for Friends, with our emphasis on the direct, unmediated approach to God.

It is a faculty of the soul which 'recognises' its own like, and in recognising, responds. In other words, our inner being is like (made in the image of) God's inner being. There is within us just such a unity, or empty space, or nothing-at-all, or silence as there is in God. Have you ever visited a house which looks small on the outside, but seems much bigger inside? That is what this space within is like.

There is in us, at the absolute core of our being, something which is as mysterious, unlimited and image-free as the absolute core of God's being. George Fox referred to it as 'that of God within'. Eckhart says that this depth of the soul is so far within, so hidden, so 'secret' (that is, so far from anything we can imagine or describe) that not even God can enter.

QUOTES

He means a God bent out of shape by the weight of the images we have heaped upon him/her. But the God who is free of all ideas, conceptions and images is already in there.

Eckhart uses different names for this deep of the soul. He calls it a 'castle', the 'ground' of the soul, and, most often, the 'spark' (*funkelin*) in the soul. There, he says, where we are nothing but true self, true silence, we encounter true God; and behold, they are compatible.

*   *   *

It seems right at this point in my personal chapters to step aside from the theory and relate it to my personal experience. They are otherwise at best an anthology of good ideas, at worst a set of notions. So I would like to say something about how the Eckhartian description of the silence at the heart of God has become real for me.

I can trace my love of silence back more than forty years, to when I was ten. I remember the strange sense I had of *rightness* when the playground whistle brought two hundred juniors to a silent standstill. We stood like statues, until a second whistle sent us (still silent) into class lines. At a third whistle we walked to our class-rooms. I can still hear the sound of shoes on the asphalt, accentuated by that silence.

Thus I suppose it is not surprising that after a winding path through Anglicanism, Methodism, nothing at all, Anglicanism again, and nothing at all again, I found my way among Friends. Like many another, I sank into my first Meeting for Worship with a profound sense of homecoming. I was fortunate in the Meeting I joined: it had (and still has, twenty years later) a real sense of the living God. Not all Meetings do. I draw my sense of what a gathered Meeting can be from my home Meeting.

So I came from the absence of sound in the school playground to the silence which is the matrix for the presence of God. I experienced this sense of presence particularly strongly one Sunday about ten years ago. It was a silent meeting for a while, and I was seeking a sense of God. Suddenly—truly suddenly—there came into my mind the words, 'Why do you keep saying you are seeking God, when God is already here?'

The sensation this produced was extraordinary—as if the room had filled up with something. I was aware of the presence of God as certainly as if a physically visible person had entered the room. There was little spoken ministry, and what there was arose out of the silence and sank back into it. I can't remember any of it. After meeting I was reluctant to speak of the experience; but I overhead someone else describing having had a similar experience during that meeting; and before long it was being agreed that this had indeed been a special meeting. I have never had this experience again, welcome as it would be, although I have certainly experienced gathered meetings since then.

The next stage of this personal story is a growing interest in Meister Eckhart. In the early 1960s I had bought and partly read some of his sermons, but subsequently forgotten all about them. My interest was re-aroused in the 1980s when I became interested in mysticism, so that by 1985 I was beginning to read him again. I found his teaching immensely exciting, for three reasons: his intellectual scope and brilliance; his Zen-like teaching method, breaking through the intellectual framework by the use of paradoxical images; and the idea of the nothingness of God. I found this latter a profound relief, though an intellectual rather than inner one.

During 1990 I came with great sadness to accept that I was no longer 'experiencing the presence of God' in Meeting for Worship, or anywhere else. Recent events in my life—and it is as painful to record this as to remember it—made me begin to wonder whether a problem of conscience lay between me and

the Presence, though I do have to say that I could not find any of
the tell-tale symptoms of that. Then, at an international Quaker
Women's conference in the summer of that year, two things happened, close together, both in Meetings for Worship.

The first was the recognition—or perhaps the internalisa-
tion—of the fact that if God is, as Eckhart says, nothing-at-all,
then clearly one cannot expect 'experiences' (and in fact, this is
just what Eckhart says). This, I perceived, was not to deny the
reality of my earlier experience of God's presence. That was
genuine, and I want to emphasize that. But I had now moved into
another kind of experience of God, another mode; and in that
mode, which was a journey towards the nothingness of God, the
very absence of 'experience' was itself a road sign. I experienced this insight with the same intensity that I had experienced
the Presence, and I would describe it as a religious experience;
knowing something as George Fox would say 'experimentally'.

This was perhaps the ground for what happened next—two or
three days later—also in a Meeting for Worship. There had been
a great deal of spoken ministry from Friends of the programmed
Quaker tradition, and Friends from the unprogrammed tradition,
accustomed to longer pauses and lengthy silences, were feeling
some distress.

Gradually it became clear to me that I was being called upon
to minister not words, but silence. I was reluctant, fearing that
the Friends who had already given spoken ministry might interpret this as a hurtful rebuke, which I did not intend. Yet there
was no doubt in my mind that I must find a way to release into
the room the silence that was rising in me like a volcanic erup-
tion. When I was finally driven to my feet I was quaking, and the
words with which I tried to explain what was happening to me
were not (I now think) appropriate. But when I reached the end
of the words and stood mute, what I felt pass through me was, I
believe, that silence of God described by Meister Eckhart. It was

not the *absence* of anything, but the presence of nothing—nothing. This was affirmed by Friends who spoke to me afterwards. I was afraid at the time, and even now that fear is very real to me: fear both of the presence of God, and of the absolute void which passed through me that morning.

My experience seems to me to raise two questions. The first derives from the feeling of no longer being aware of the presence of God. How are we to know whether this is in fact an experience of the nothing-at-all at the heart of God?

The second question is: are there any means we can employ for getting nearer to it?

In answer to the first question, Eckhart offers some very helpful advice. First, since the spark in the soul is hidden, and God unknowable by normal human means, experience of God can happen in secret, so secretly one does not even know it is happening. What one *will* perceive is the result (and I shall have more to say about that in the next chapter). One does not see the moon exert its influence on the sea: one only sees the sandy shore appear and disappear.

Second, we should all be deeply suspicious of Religious Experience, especially if it is special. God is no more to be found in one place than another, one feeling than another. If in doubt, trust what is ordinary, normal, unless there are compelling reasons to do otherwise. Moses did not experience God as a burning bush: that was merely a road-sign. The experience to which it pointed the way was never fully articulated because it couldn't be, and we know of it only because its results changed the course of history.

I don't think Eckhart is denying the validity of religious experience; rather, questioning the importance of abnormal manifestations. Like many a mystic before and since, he is sceptical about visions and fervent feelings on the path towards God:

the sense that one's spiritual life is dead is not necessarily an indication that God is absent, or dead, or even that nothing is happening.

My second question is whether there is a means we can employ for moving nearer to the silence of God. Eckhart's key word in answering this is *abgescheidenheit*—a state of detachment, non-attachment, non-possessiveness, a learnt ability not to be programmed or dominated by any desire.

I suppose it is obvious that people are healthier, more whole, more themselves, when not in the grip of obsessional habits. For example, they can be so utterly possessed by the habit of smoking that cigaretteless they can think of nothing else (I'll give it up when I have had just one more?). Perhaps it is less obvious that Friends can become possessed by the habit of Quaker committees (I'll agree to come off next year/in the next triennium?): but it is a syndrome well known to anyone who has ever had to ask long-standing members of committees to retire.

Even less obvious, but possibly more widely true, is the fact that people can be possessed by what they like to describe as a desire for God. This would seem very spiritual—but in truth the desire that possesses them may well be for a God made in their own image, tied wholly to their human, temporal existence, and modelled out of their own answers to their needs. We all certainly do have needs, and God can certainly help us deal with them; but this often happens in ways we experience as disappointing, we even claim that God didn't answer our prayers, because we are addicted to the image of a particular kind of God who will produce a particular set of answers.

We Friends are as addicted to 'our' sort of God as any other group is: kindly, tolerant, indifferent to intellectual rigour, self-effacing, quiet. How many of us would ever think of such a God as angry—yet love sometimes is, and must be, very angry indeed . . .

Clearly, we are never going to reach the imageless centre of God if we are unable to recognise our images of God for what they are: images, not the thing itself. Of course, we need images: they are deeply rooted in our psychology, they express real meaning to us, and they can help us to grow spiritually when they extend our understanding and our experience. But we must not be possessed by them.

I have remembered over many years a scientist (though not his name, unfortunately) who, in one of a series of television programmes about science and religion, said that he only believed in God because God exists, not because God is love, or any of the other nice things you could say of him. It was, said the scientist, a bonus that God was well-disposed towards the human race. That was Eckhart's detachment from images.

Eckhart is *not* saying (and nor am I) that we must immediately abandon all images in a sort of mindless iconoclasm. His own context as a faithful member of his church, as a Dominican teacher and preacher, and his very vivid use of images (such as spark, castle, 'catching God naked in his dressing-room') tell us that Eckhart himself was well aware of the value, even the necessity at some points, of images. But we must become strong and brave and detached enough to review them from time to time, however painful that process may be.

In fact, the pain we experience when called upon to do this exercise in any meaningful way, is proof of the image-clinging nature of our faith. One of my favourite stories is of the man who fell over a cliff, but managed to clutch hold of a small bush. It was pulling loose, and he shouted 'Is there anybody up there who can help me?' A great voice came from above: 'Let go: I will catch you.' There was a pause, and then the man said 'Is there anyone else up there I can speak to?'[6]

'Let go,' says Eckhart. Falling is lovely. You will arrive inside your true self, and that is where God is; that is where God *already* is, patiently waiting for you.

What is more, this detachment is not only the *means* towards the inner silence of God: it is also the *result* of that journey. It follows that the detachment is nothing like indifference, either towards one's self (that being the very precious place where one experiences God) or towards others and the creation. On the contrary, those who are truly detached are people of great passion and commitment. It is simply that they are not possessed by anything or anyone. They have learnt to let go.

I have tried to outline what seems to me to be an area of Eckhart's teaching that has relevance for Friends. He emphasises the un-map-ability, or silence, of God's inner being. He tries to show that the un-map-ability, or silence, is also in us; and that like is drawn to like. The path is one of detachment—learning not to be possessed by anything, not even ideas about God. The goal (for which we were created) is encounter and relationship with this being in the most profound depths of ourselves. Religion may help with this, mainly because it preserves what others have learnt along the way, but also because it should provide an appropriate (safe) framework in which we can review the images we use. It can, on the other hand, hinder, when it confuses preservation of what has been learnt with providing a framework for learning. In any case, the God Eckhart knows and tries to speak of is far beyond any particular religion, and may just as well be found in the secular world—though, of course, some religions and some aspects of secularity may be more helpful, truthful than others.

What does all this mean for Friends? Does it have anything to say about ministry in Meeting for Worship, and in the everyday world?

CHAPTER 6

Being and Doing

There has been a great deal of emphasis in this book upon the search for the true self: not so much the inner journey as the journey inwards. We have emphasised this because in our experience some Friends are inclined to regard attention to self as selfish: 'navel-gazing', 'taking one's own temperature', 'let sleeping dragons lie', are all phrases we have heard more than once in the course of our work among Friends. This inhibition owes much to a pre-seventeenth century Puritan tradition that by-passed early Quakerism but was added to it at a later stage. George Fox had no such inhibition: passage after passage of the Journal shows him paying the most penetrating attention to his inner consciousness, recognising its dragons and confronting them, making them useful in his own spiritual development. He describes what happened to him in 1647 thus:

> Yet I was under great temptations sometimes, and my inward sufferings were heavy; but I could find none to open my condition to but the Lord alone, unto whom I cried night and day. And I went back into Nottinghamshire, and there the Lord shewed me that the natures of those things which were hurtful without were within, in the hearts and minds of wicked men. The natures of dogs, swine, vipers, of Sodom and Egypt, Pharaoh, Cain, Ishmael, Esau, etc. The natures of these I saw within, though people had been looking without.[1]

However, no one could describe George Fox as navel-gazing; there can hardly have been a more active traveller, preacher and organizer than Fox in the history of Christianity. So I come now to the subject of ministry as action in the world.

Eckhart's 'model' of God has something to say here, expressed in another aspect of his teaching. If it is true to say of Fox that he was one of the most active missionaries it is possible to imagine, this is also true of Eckhart, who spent a large part of his life travelling through Europe in the service of his Order. How does it happen that a man who is claiming that the inner being of God is absolute stillness, absolute silence, and that our true inner being is an image of that, could at the same time be rushing about Europe, talking in the energetic way reflected in his sermons?

The answer lies in his model of God. Deep within, God is one, still, silent, neither going out nor coming in, nor planning to do so. But the truth about God also includes the fact that out of the abyss of nothingness, no-thing-ness, God 'melts and boils' as Eckhart puts it[2]—erupts in an act of continuous creativity. The act of creation requires an activity ('Holy Spirit') and that which is created ('Son'); and it is this which is traditionally formulated as the Trinity. Out of the Trinity the universe and all its creatures draw their being. This also explains how it is that although humanity's destination, spiritually, is the experience of the inner being of God in the imageless depths of the individual soul, it is also possible to experience God in other modes out in the world.

What Eckhart's model of God suggests is that the activity of God in the world, as creator, sustainer, lover, is so to speak fuelled, or empowered, by that silent inner being, to which God as it were, returns or withdraws. The going-forth is exactly balanced by a withdrawing-to-within. I have to *picture* this as being one event followed by another: but it is not. God's going-forth is (oh lovely paradox!) completely simultaneous with God's withdrawing and God's inaction.

The true source, then, of God's creative action is the inner being of God. It follows from this that *our* true source of creative action can only be the absolute stillness 'within' God, the absolute silence, which is also within us.

It is obvious that the best, the most effective, action in the world is God's own action—or the closest that God's human agent can get to this. A Christian might want to cite the human life and death of Jesus as an example of this truth. If we want to be effective (and there are many other words we could substitute for 'effective', such as 'good', 'creative', 'healing', or even 'obedient') we have to align ourselves to the activity of God, become part of it. This is done by agreeing to be drawn into God's going-forth and, therefore and inescapably, into God's withdrawing. We have to become part of God's process.

We, as creatures living in a universe governed by what we call time, will not experience the two directions of this process as simultaneous, at least at first. We will need to speak of times of withdrawal and concentration on what is within, balanced by times of action in the world. But it is the willingness to be drawn into the process that empowers us, that gives us the energy to do the work of God in the world.

There is no source of true action in the world, except the secret silence of God.

However, I am certainly not wanting to claim that the secret silence of God is experienced only in a Quaker Meeting for Worship (which is often far from silent even when there is a total absence of spoken words), nor is it experienced only by Quakers, or Christians, or religious people. Our late Friend Ted Randall, who was much involved in ecumenical activity, used to fulminate about what he called Quaker triumphalism—as if we had invented silence, and had a monopoly on it. On the other hand, Friends have paid particular attention to silence, and the question is whether Friends are being called upon to play any special part in the drawing of the whole human race into the God-process.

Meanwhile, however, there are two more things I would like to say before we can go on to think about a specifically Quaker ministry.

The first is negative. It involves the converse of being drawn into the movement of God (into silence and into action). If people refuse to be drawn into the uncharted inner being of God, into the dark, into the silence, they are likely, unconsciously, to feel guilty and anxious about the refusal, and they will usually try to compensate for those guilty feelings by being extremely active in the world.

Further, a refusal to be drawn into God is also a refusal to be drawn into self, and the result will be (to use a modern psychological term) alienation from true self. This will leave one vulnerable to being possessed by the arbitrary demands of the outward self, the ego, or the image imposed by others, or by temporal circumstances. That *feels* like living in a hostile or unreasonably demanding universe, although in truth the hostility and the demands come from within.

Such persons are driven by what someone recently called 'the lethal energy of the hidden agenda', where everything supposedly done for others has a secondary motive dictated by an unacknowledged, or even unrecognised, inward drive. This drive is fuelled by a voracious and obsessive appetite to destroy, by consuming, everything that seems to threaten the ego. Desperate extremes of this syndrome can be seen in history. Hitler and Stalin are safely distant examples. All dictators suffer from it, and it may well be why (as Lord Acton once said) all power tends to corrupt. Macbeth is a literary example. Kronos, the Greek god who ate his children, is a mythological example. Religious fanatics sometimes come into this category.

But—and this is really the point—it is present in all of us. This is why learning to let go is of paramount importance in our spiritual growth. Here is what George Fox had to say about it:

'Friends, whatever ye are addicted to, the tempter will come in that thing; and when he can trouble you, then he gets advantage over you, and then you are gone. Stand still in that which is pure, after ye see yourselves; and then mercy comes in. After thou seest thy thoughts, and the temptations, do not think, but submit; and then power comes. Stand still in that which shows and discovers; and then doth strength immediately come. And stand still in the Light, and submit to it, and the other will be hush'd and gone; and then content comes.'[3]

The second thing to be said is positive. One of the surest signs that a soul is being fed by encounter at the centre is a renewal of images. It may sound very strange to be saying on the one hand that the essence of God and of individuals is pure silence and imagelessness, and then to be saying on the other that a sign of this silence and imagelessness is a renewal of images; but it is so. The teaching of all the great mystics—the Buddha and Jesus included—brims over with new and renewed images, images falling over one another, contradicting one another, acting upon each other as complementary colours do in an Impressionist painting, creating a sense of light and power. Artists and writers also create images, and it is possible to recognise the authenticity of such new images even when they seem strange or bizarre—of course, because there is that within us all which recognises the source.

Being and doing are intimately linked. Being in God's silence is necessary for true action in the world. What we are called upon to do can only spring authentically from the secret silence.

The failure to turn to the silence of God, it seems to me, explains the sporadic difficulties encountered by all religious groups over stewardship of time and resources—money, goods, or people. The Religious Society of Friends is no exception to this, and has recently had to wrestle with re-balancing increased needs at home and abroad with decreasing resources of money, time and people willing to give service. This tension appears across a wide spectrum of situations, from the problems of an ageing local Friends Meeting in a town with increasing social problems, to the difficulties of sustaining (or withdrawing from) desperately needed health and education projects world-wide. There is no failure of conscience here, no hardening of hearts, no 'compassion fatigue'—only dwindling resources and escalating needs. In this situation we are all dogged by guilty feelings (often a sign of the hidden agenda described above) and are less and less able to refrain from action. How then can we properly discern the right allocation of those resources we do have?

Part of the answer is debate: the sharing of ideas and opinions, the assessment of resources and the sensitive and compassionate review of needs. But the other part of the answer, given the drive of those guilty feelings, is much more difficult to hear, because it demands willingness to seem to do nothing while the silence of God is sought, perhaps for quite a long time. Yet without this it is quite certain no lasting answer can be reached.

This seeking of the silence is surely what we Friends mean, or should mean, when we say of our Meetings for Business that neither majority opinion nor consensus is being sought, but the will of God. It is thus of crucial importance to our work in the world that we become able to detach ourselves and allow ourselves to be drawn into the silence and inactivity of God; that we enter a state of 'being' so that our 'doing' (when or even if it is required of us) may spring from the only true source of creative action.

PART IV

WHAT ARE THE IMPLICATIONS?

CHAPTER 7

The Shaping Spirit

What is the ministry of the Religious Society of Friends to the world? More specifically, what is the ministry of Friends in London Yearly Meeting in the Decade of Evangelism? These are very large questions, but Friends can only respond: 'Here is our space. We minister from where we are and from what we are.'

It seems to us that Friends minister from and through silence and images: the still centre and the dynamic process. In both of these they affirm their experience of God and of the agency of the Holy Spirit.

Francis Hall identifies the unique contribution Friends have to offer thus: 'Quakerism asserts the primacy of the Spirit in all true religion'[1] Further, he sees in Quakerism the potential for 'developing a clearer understanding of evangelical spirituality. Quakerism is both; it is evangelical and it is spiritual'.[2]

> The discovery by Friends that a change in the heart takes place when one comes into the living experience of God must be reasserted and offered to those who are involved in social struggles. Deeper than force, deeper than social pressures, deeper than psychology, deeper than the commitment of the will, even when it is a religiously oriented will, is the transformation of the very nature of humankind that takes place when it comes into that life and power which takes away the occasion of all war.[3]

What paths might there be to those depths where people can be transformed, and from where they can transform? We believe that Friends need fully to experience their images, examine

them and test them, and find and own their silence. As the
images and silence open them to God they will be empowered to
become people who can listen and people who can speak.

The earth was without form and void: and darkness was
upon the face of the deep; and the Spirit of God was moving
over the face of the waters.[4]

The opening chapter of *Genesis* describes the agency of the
Holy Spirit bringing the shapes of creation out of chaos. The
stages in this process can be seen as separating, identifying and
naming. This works as a model for the process of the human
creative imagination. In the words of S.T. Coleridge:

The primary imagination I hold to be the living power and
prime agent of all human perception, and as a repetition in the
finite mind of the eternal act of creation in the infinite I AM.[5]

The human creative process resembles God's creative process because the Holy Spirit operates in and through the imagination. God's living power, like the 'secret ministry of frost'[6]
comes in the silence and the darkness, and it is unacknowledged
by us until, 'imagination bodies forth the forms of things
unknown.'[7]

For us as Friends, affirming 'the primacy of the Spirit', it is
especially important that we do not stultify the Spirit by fencing
it in with notions or swamping it with unacknowledged emotions. Space must be allowed for the Spirit to operate, in ourselves, in our Meetings for Worship, in our relationships and our
activities in the world.

We all need to be educated in a kind of school of imagery, a
school of the Holy Spirit where we allow the birth of images and
understand their connection with traditional, inherited images.
We need to learn to be discriminating in identifying the truths
they bring to us, using them in transformed lives.

What follows is a kind of syllabus for such experiential learning, a school for our own ministry of images, tutored by the shaping Spirit.

Images from our traditions

'All art is an attempt to manifest the Face of the God of Life.'
Cecil Collins.[8]

George Gorman described really seeing a painting by Vermeer as a 'truly worshipful experience'. He added, 'I know that my ordinary acts of seeing and observation have been sharpened by that experience.'[9] In an interview, Iris Murdoch talked about the connection between art and religion. When experiencing a great work of art one can, she says,

> . . . have extraordinary feelings of exaltation . . . the feeling that your own shadowy ideas, your cobweb of anxieties and so on, is parted like a curtain, and you look into a world created by some great genius, himself inspired by forces beyond. Suddenly, it's an image of the death of egoism. Religion is about the death of the ego. The ego disappears and you see the world with absolute vividness and clarity.[10]

Art extends experience. It begins by operating within the reality normally thought of as familiar, but it is not limited to that reality. Art makes a space for new images and new experiences which our own experience has excluded.

In using the word art, we are not, of course, limiting our reference to visual art. Other people's stories and their experiences in novels, plays, poetry and music also operate through the imagination, offering vicarious experience and insight.

One of the mysteries of life is memorably expressed by the poet Gerard Manley Hopkins. He asks what he finds when he looks inside himself:

When I consider my self-being, my consciousness and feeling

of myself, that taste of myself, of *I* and *me* above and in all things, which is more distinctive than the taste of ale or alum, more distinctive than the smell of walnut leaf or camphor, and is incommunicable by any means to another man (as when I was a child I used to ask myself: what must it be like to be someone else?)[11]

That child's question can never be answered. The nearest anyone can approach is through stories, novels, poetry and the other arts which help us to enter another person's consciousness.

Appreciation and practice of the arts and crafts relate at the very deepest level to our inner being. The artist and the maker in search of truth venture deeper than most of us dare into the paradoxes and mysteries of human experience—joy, pain, our delicate and now threatened relationship with the natural world, our fraught and miraculous relationships with each other and with God. Artists make the journey into that interior deliberately, regarding it as their calling to discover and reveal inner pattern and meaning, or warn us when these things are fractured or even missing. They often do this without counting the cost to themselves; and in the apparently inchoate darkness or blinding light of that experience they create a new way of communicating their unique vision.

This can be compared with the utterances of the prophets, the mystics and other great leaders whom we recognise as being empowered, as being channels of the Spirit. From their insights succeeding generations can draw sustenance. We have offered two examples in Meister Eckhart and Julian of Norwich. These artists and mystics take risks in exploring the dark, strange places, and they return with images for our transformation.

Images inherited from cultural and religious traditions are able to nurture us as individuals and corporately in our Meetings for Worship. There is, however, work laid on us if we are to have access to our inheritance. We need to know the sacred texts which are part of our sacred tradition and which give us the sense of being a people. There are great openings for us in Jesus's teaching method which deals not with facts and theories, not with answers, but with questions, stories and images for our imaginations.

We all need to reclaim our traditional metaphors. For example, being 'born again' resonates with a certain kind of narrow biblical certainty. When Brenda joined Friends, however, this was the metaphor she needed to express her sense of beginning anew. The parable of the sheep and the goats is another example of a parable we need to reclaim from evangelical certainties about our destination in the after life. It is a profound mystical insight into our state of being now, of what is happening all the time we minister to each other—or omit to do so.

There are also great openings for us in our Quaker sacred texts. Fox and Penington especially, used images in an original and startling way. Penington described Friends in Meeting as 'living stones of the Meeting House' and 'an heap of living coals warming one another.'[12] Fox used the seed not so much as a naturalistic image of growth, but as contained power and his use of the image of light was not exactly bland, seeing it as a searching beam, raking our darkness and bringing understanding and self-knowledge.

Images from our own experience

Artists, prophets and mystics make a map of that part of the inner labyrinth they have explored, and say which way might lead towards truth, and which might not. However, all of us are capable of learning in this way, by actively participating in the arts ourselves. Indeed it is imperative that we do so. It has little to do with being 'arty', and everything to do with the search for truth. It is, after all, what we are all doing in Meeting for Worship; we are seeking God in the deepest places we dare to reach, and trying to share with our Friends what we have found. And, as each of us has a unique vision of the truth, if we do not dare to find it and declare what we have seen, a part of the truth will never be known.

There are many ways in which the arts can help us to find and own our own truth.

We can grow by exploring and using our stories. Let us take the image that each of us is 'in our own story'. We are all at different chapters, and the plots, characters and settings vary. The question is: Who is writing my story? What is its controlling idea, or theme? If I have a major transforming experience, how will this affect the plot? As Christians and Quakers we would hope to answer that ambition does not control us, nor possessiveness, nor materialism. We would hope that none of these controls us, but that God controls us. Each of our stories has a controlling idea which is its belief structure. We hope that truly includes God.

In *Appleseed*[13] weekends the response activities, which take the place of discussion, are arts based. One of them is called a words workshop and this begins with simple word association games which lead participants into the process of catching the flow of their consciousness and recognising the stops, starts and connections which lie buried. By allowing the apparent randomness of the flickering mind to be captured in this way, it is possible to begin to discover what is waiting to be brought into the light. Subsequent activities in a words workshop use archetypal images in carefully structured but intensive exercises which are designed to ambush the controlling mind and facilitate the discovery and acknowledgement of what is really being thought and felt.

Another response activity is spontaneous painting which is for most people a very releasing and healing experience. This kind of painting liberates people from worrying about technique and accuracy and enables them to make discoveries about their inner selves and also about their own innate creativity. It is an attempt to use colour, shape, line and texture to express what reality is—not what people ought to feel, but what they do feel. For many people this kind of painting has involved some painful recognitions, but it has also brought them to a deeper awareness of the action of the Holy Spirit in their lives.

Similar processes can be seen when weaving, collage or clay are used for expressive purposes. People might, for example, make their 'inner judge', or their inner paralytic—the immobilised, frozen, handicapped self. Or they weave patterns of their life as it is, or has been, and how they wish it would, and could be. All of these activities use the various artistic and craft media to create images for self discovery and for God discovery.[14]

Images in Worship

In Chapter 2 we have already said a great deal about our Quaker worship, its risks, its pitfalls, its huge possibilities. Friends said in their response to the Lima text: 'Absence of form and of structure no more guarantee depth and spirituality of worship than do their presence.'[15]

In Friends' Meetings the visual structure is of the square or circle facing inwards. This is archetypal and connects with other, ancient traditions as well as being a symbolic representation of Friends' beliefs—that our focus is God, not one of us as priest or leader, and that in worship we turn inwards to the deep centre.

In accepting and recognising Quaker rejection of outward forms of symbols or rites in many respects, we should take care not to ignore this most basic image of the sacred centre of our Meeting for Worship.

What do we have in the centre as our special images of our dependence upon the Holy Spirit? We have a table holding flowers and our Christian and Quaker sacred books. These books remind us that we are a people, a church with a communal sacred history of the way in which others received and communicated the spirit of God; they connect us with our tradition, our living past and our inherited images. The flowers are a focus for being here in our present sacred time together; they speak silently and wordlessly of being here now, budding patiently under the eye of God.[16]

Are these visual images which speak to us of and from the deep centre? It has been suggested that we should have nothing at all in the centre of the meeting room, as even these are too directive. Others would like the freedom to have a greater diversity of symbols to lead Friends into more adventurous worship.

Our unique form of Quaker worship makes us very open to images. Meeting for Worship has been described as the 'workshop of the ministry' or 'laboratory of the spirit'. Of course we are not all acknowledged poets, but we each have our own experience of images which are towards God, which point us to the mystery.

In the silence and the waiting images come. Sometimes it seems an image for us alone, at other times we feel the Spirit moving us to share it. The following are two examples from one Meeting. A Friend described seeing cheeses maturing at Cheddar. It was explained to her that the characteristic flavour of a mature Cheddar comes from the passive months it spends in the right temperature, humidity and light. She felt that in Meeting we were exposed to the right conditions for the maturing of our souls. We had to wait, absorbing the experience, allowing ourselves to be worked upon. Another Friend described the experience of developing photographs in his dark room. Gradually images took shape out of the formless void. The dark room of the photographer was experienced as the dark mystery at the heart of Meeting for Worship. We were all in a process of becoming and waiting to be brought into focus.

In both of these offerings of ministry there was a linking of everyday experience with the deeper reaches of worship. It is important that this connection with ordinary experience is maintained and that there is not a self-consciously 'poetic' concept of what images should be. Images can derive from an urban landscape including factories, shops, parks, or from modern transport using the graceful landing of an aeroplane, lorry headlights on a dark night, the operation of windscreen wipers in driving rain, or high-speed trains rushing past each other.

Sometimes, however, one traditional image can be the central focus for the whole Meeting. We recall one such example where the Quaker image of the seed was the starting point and it had its own spiritual growth in a deeply gathered Meeting. The ministry included: personal experience directly related to the image through an apple tree in a Friend's garden; joy and hope at future exciting opportunities for one Friend; sadness at human suffering experienced by another; references to George Fox and Jesus's parables; insight from one of the mystics and finally a welcoming of the dark, unknown times for the hidden periods of growing. This ministry brought in the more practised ministers and the less confident, including one Friend who had not ministered for ten years! It also did not prevent the offering of one very deeply felt piece of ministry which had apparently only a tenuous link with the image, but which grew its own connectedness. We felt the Spirit moving among us, binding us and nurturing us.

This kind of sharing and relating to an image is in the Spirit, and is very different from Meetings which are centred around a theme or concept, which are more often in the head.

Images and Prayer

To whom do you pray? What is your image of the God who receives your prayers?

We Friends are often very sheepish and uneasy when discussing prayer. As always, we can readily say what we reject:

the repeating of set forms of prayer Sunday after Sunday; the automatic adding of 'Amen' to lengthy extempore prayer structured and led by an appointed minister. We reject the conditioned response. In abandoning this, do we pray at all? How can images help Friends to find a way of Quaker prayer?

Some approaches to prayer take passages from the Bible (or other sacred texts, or spiritual writings) and use them as an imaginative exercise of prayer in which the images in the passage become vivid and alive and open the spirit to God. These approaches have a long history in the Christian tradition, the *Lectio Divina* or sacred reading going back to the very first Benedictine monasteries, while the Ignatian exercises were initiated in the Renaissance period.

In all prayer it is helpful, and indeed necessary in the early stages, to have images to help make our prayer less self-willed and more an openness before God.

The image used by Julian of Norwich about prayer, 'I am the ground of your beseeching', has been mentioned earlier, in Chapter Four. St. Teresa of Avila compares the degrees of mystical prayer with four ways of watering a garden: firstly, drawing the water up by hand as from a deep well, demanding a great deal of human effort; secondly, things get easier as more water comes with less human effort; thirdly, as the mind ceases its efforts it is as if a little river ran through the garden; finally it is as if God himself watered the garden with his rain. St. John of the Cross uses the image of a log burning on a fire to show the stages of purgation, illumination and union in contemplative prayer. In George Herbert's sonnet[17] prayer is a multiplicity of images and a glimpse of insight.

Isaac Penington also sees prayer as a uniting of the soul with God.

'Prayer is the true breathing of the child to the Father which begat it.' Here the breathing image is helpful in understanding prayer as wordless, inarticulate, but also natural and inevitable. 'Prayer is a gift,' says Penington, 'out of the will of the creature.'[18]

Zen meditation also has an initial focus on the image of breathing to still the mind and take the meditator onward and inward to the place of imagelessness. In Christian contemplative prayer the tradition has been to use another kind of symbol, a mantra, or a visual image, to help reach the darkness and emptiness of unknowing. It is this kind of prayer which is usually considered to have a radical transforming power. For Ann and Barry Ulanov, 'Prayer . . . is primary speech. It is that primordial discourse in which we assert, however clumsily or eloquently, our own being.' Their book is an exploration of prayer as a dynamic, basic, sometimes wordless speech operating in the depths of the self.[19]

Which of these images speaks to your condition? Or do you have other images to lead you into prayer? Quakers have the freedom to mine the rich traditions of the past, but also have the responsibility of testing them for truth to experience.

Communicating and Images

The Christian faith requires all of us to communicate with each other and the world at large, trying to be faithful to the truth as we have experienced it, and describing it in terms that can be understood. We Quakers try to fulfil this requirement in ministry in our Meetings for Worship, and in service among our fellow creatures; but we need to become more articulate.

Fellowship is central to our spiritual journeys; the Holy Spirit at Pentecost came to the gathered group. Although religion is partly what people do with their solitude, it is also essentially what brings individuals together to be a people, a church or, as we suggest later, a religious order.

Some images which describe our bonding are given by

Penington: 'a knitting of natures and a fellowship in the same spiritual centre,'[20] and Mary Elson, 'Blessed be the name of the Lord who hath quickened and made alive unto himself and hath knit and tyed and bundled up and hath united us together in one Spirit.'[21]

What active role can images play in communicating?

Friends already have a basic structure, which stops them from merely exchanging notions and enables them to share their experiences and their reflections upon them so that they come nearer to getting to know one another in the things which are eternal.

This exercise is called creative listening, or sometimes worship sharing. These are not identical, the main difference being that worship sharing can include prayers and direct appeals to God or the Holy Spirit as part of vocal contributions. In creative listening the focus is on carefully and fully hearing one another. In both, however, the silence between contributions, the focus on listening, sharing and upholding rather than on contradicting or interrupting and invalidating what has been said, may be symbolised by the conch or symbolic object which is in the centre of the group. She who has the conch has both her speaking and her silence protected and honoured.

In such sharing, contributions often come in the form of images, because what is taking place is not mental discussion but an opening and sharing of new insights.

Another, less familiar exercise is worship seeing and our first experience of this was in a *Gifts and Discoveries* exercise.[22] Each of us in turn sat in the centre of the group and was the focus of the whole group's loving attention. Each group member, resting a hand on the head or shoulders of the Friend in the centre, described the image or images he had about this Friend, images which expressed the Friend's stage on her spiritual journey, her needs and, above all, her gifts and potential for growth. These were written down by a kind of 'rotating' recording clerk, so that finally we each took away a card with our given images written on it. We have since heard that few *Gifts and Discoveries* groups have attempted this exercise, finding it too risky and threatening. We would commend it as a deeply affirming experience. It bonded and gathered a group which had, until then, been rather tentative and shy.

The personal image-making described earlier, using words, painting, weaving, clay, or another medium, can also be used in a similar way. Communication at a very deep level happens when members of a response activity group look with absolute loving attention at the images which others have produced.

Another way of using the imagination and releasing positive images is found in the Buddhist *Metta Bhavana* meditation where its structures encourage people fully to visualise those with whom they are in conflict, or even dislike, if they are brave enough to admit to such unFriendly feelings . . . In the course of this meditation the imagination is used to make vivid and real the quality of one's feelings for oneself, one's close friends, one's casual acquaintances and one's problem people, so that an attempt can be made to develop (*bhavana*) loving kindness (*metta*) for all, seeing that all people are equally in need. This can, perhaps, be connected with George Fox's mystical insight, his 'worship seeing' of that of God in everyone. It is also expressed in the parable of the sheep and the goats in the Gospels.

It is possible to do many good deeds and loving actions but still *feel* unloving, still feel the centre of one's being to be a lump of unleavened dough, soggy, heavy and dour. This is then far from the vision of the transformation of human nature. But living, acting and being a life of love can become more available to all of us when we see others illumined through positive images. This can only happen when we stop projecting images which are the result of our own unresolved conflicts on to other people.

*   *   *

As the 1991 London Yearly Meeting Epistle reminds us:

'Each person in prison is unique, precious, a child of God.'

We would make this an image to include all the imprisoning structures, physical, mental, emotional, social, spiritual, which prevent us from attaining Irenaeus' vision of the human being fully alive as the glory of God.

'I came,' said Jesus, 'that they may have life, and have it abundantly.'[23]

CHAPTER 8

Ministry and Silence

It is our view that turning towards the silence of God empowers creative action in the world, and that this may have a special significance for Friends. All Quakers profess to be, and most really are, deeply attached to the silence of their Meetings for Worship. There are many kinds of silence in Meeting: absence of spoken words (though not necessarily of unspoken words); expectant silence, in which Friends wait for spoken ministry; the silence that gathers round shocking news or moving personal testimony. In all these, Friends would say they are waiting for the voice of God, or the moving of the Spirit.

But what if one of God's modes is not speaking, but silence? What if Eckhart is right when he says that in the depth of God there is absolute silence? Might Friends not be called to minister this? Not minister *about* it, but minister, be the channel of, the silence itself?

It is the task of the prophet to be the voice of God in a particular situation; and much has been said about the prophetic role of the church in our tearful and distracted world. Each part of the church, and (Friends would insist) each individual, has a prophetic role, a calling to communicate God. Might not the Religious Society of Friends be called to utter the silence of God?

There are religious orders within the Catholic and Orthodox parts of the church which 'specialise' in silence: men and women who have responded to a call to step permanently aside from ordinary daily life to become channels to and from the silence of God. This turning aside is often painful for the called individual (contrary to common belief), and the silent convent or monastery is no place for an escapist. Many of the delights of the world seem much more delightful when you do not have them; and monastic literature is full of images of temptation—the Temptations of St Antony, for example. The life of enclosed silence is difficult and demanding, confronting the individual with the daunting addiction we all have for trivia and distractions. Archbishop Michael Ramsey once said that we all seem to long for time to be with God, but when we get it, the first thing we learn is how little we really do want it. The path through the monastery or convent towards silence requires self-discipline, abundant love for self and others, and courage. Further, it is not about self-salvation, but about connecting God and world—or, perhaps, witnessing to the connection.

What happens within those walls is, broadly speaking, three-fold. There is the spiritual development of the individual by means of a path whose toughness would daunt most of us. This is not a pursuit of the gratification of the ego, nor a fleeing from the horrors, demands and temptations of the world; but rather a facing of these things and an attempt to see them for what they really are. Strangely enough, it is an attempt to become oneself, which is what God requires one to be.

Then, there is prayer for others. A journalist who visited an enclosed order during research for an article said that the nuns within knew more about world affairs than did most people outside. The nuns understood that prayer must be intelligent and fully informed. The monasteries of Christendom are power-houses of such prayer, and it can be a consolation in the course of a sleepless night to know that somewhere such prayer is going on, and that one may join in, or simply be upheld by its existence.

Third, there is the physical providing of a silent haven, usually in the form of a group or individual retreat, for those who have come to know they need it. A number of Friends have reaped the benefit of this hospitality of the spirit, for while they may not always be able to relate to the forms and structures in which Catholics and Orthodox express their experience of God, they relate very well to the experience behind the expression; and they know a good silence when they hear it. Such Friends remain, however, a minority; and it would probably be true to say that most are still suspicious of the retreat from the world and the unfamiliar (or, sometimes, all too familiar) forms, structures, and images.

Nonetheless, there are similarities between the Religious Society of Friends and the silent orders of the church. At the "Equipping for Ministry" Conference at Woodbrooke and Westhill Colleges in 1990, the Roman Catholic observer invited to attend was a nun, Sr Anne McDowell, former Director of the Centre for Adult Religious Education at St. Mary's College, Twickenham. She said:

> I feel heartened and encouraged by the corporate witness of the Society of Friends at this conference to the importance of *attentiveness* to the Spirit and one another. The Society of Friends seems more like another religious order, rather than a denomination, in the depth of its considerations.[1]

The comment has remained with the writers of this book, and now leads us to ask this question: is the Religious Society of Friends being called to a ministry of silence—not inside an enclosure, nor through a monastic lifestyle, but in the world and through distinctively Quaker lives?

We believe we can see three ways in which a ministry of silence might express itself.

Havens of silence

The first way of offering a ministry of silence would require Friends to do what they have always done, which is to provide havens of silence for all, regardless of belief, orientation or race.

Sunday by Sunday, and during the week when a Meeting has the resources to do so, our Meetings for Worship at their best have offered a blessed absence of irrelevant words and images, together with spoken ministry and images that flow from experience of God and speak directly spirit to spirit. The silence is not the barren, dead silence in which no one can think of anything to say, nor the refusal to speak which is now associated with Quietism.

Recently a Friend spoke in Meeting for Worship of how, one Sunday morning some weeks previously, she had driven a hundred and fifty miles in a car that threatened all the way to break down, and had to be treated very gently. She arrived at Meeting for Worship very late, in an extremely frayed condition. But, she said, the moment she walked into the room she could feel the presence of the silence, and healing began.

Nothing could be less dead than the silence of God: as we have tried to suggest, it is the very crucible of healing and creation.

We have spoken earlier of the rebirth of images in Meeting for Worship, suggesting that this is a ministry Friends have to offer the world. Now we are saying that Friends also have the true silence of Meeting for Worship to offer—not the absence of words, nor even the listening silence, but the breaking through of the absolute silence of God; and here there is a need to learn to listen more attentively to the silence itself, so that meetings can discern more readily the arrival of the silence of God.

In truth, it is often the silence as much as the spoken ministry for which visitors come to Meeting for Worship, and at which they marvel. It may be the first time they have experienced something Friends would say is already deep within each person: that of God, and within that, God's absolute silence.

We are certainly *not* calling for wholly silent meetings, though these may happen from time to time. It is the Holy Spirit who should decide what happens in Meeting, not Friends. But what we *are* saying is that both absence and presence of words (or other forms of communication in adventurous worship) must be a witness to our taking part in the going-forth and withdrawing-to-centre of God: true spoken ministry arises out of our co-operation in that process.

Normally others in the world-wide church show forth the creative dance of God in the world, the glories of colour and pattern and shape, which also come from the silence. Perhaps it is for Friends to minister the silence itself.

An extension of this ministry might be to encourage others to learn that they can do likewise. For example, it is the experience of many Friends involved in ecumenical activities that clergy from other traditions sometimes underestimate the capacity of their congregations to seek silence together. They frequently say that five minutes (or even two) is the most that can be managed. This misapprehension seems to arise because the first few moments of congregational silence are fidgety; but of course, so are the first moments of even the most gathered Meeting for Worship. Sharing the experience of ordinary people being silent together for a whole hour is something Friends can offer with the confidence of three hundred years of experience.

We believe that the ministry of silence has an important part to play in the evolution of the people of God as a whole, certainly in the Christian tradition, and possibly beyond it—though we do both feel that Friends probably have more to learn about silence from some of the other faiths than to teach. Would any Friends think they knew more than a Zen Buddhist Master such as Thich Nhat Hanh about the Absolute Silence?

This book is being written during the early years of the Decade of Evangelism, towards which some Friends have displayed a certain indifference, if not positive hostility. There is a long-standing debate among Friends as to whether the Religious

Society of Friends is Christian, and what might be meant by that term anyway. It is not surprising, then, that we do not feel ourselves called to the kind of public preaching about Jesus sometimes associated with the term 'evangelism'. But is there some other way in which Friends could, without betraying their traditions, actually be evangelical?

The answer, we would suggest, is yes, but not in the normal sense of the word. The Apostle Paul had it right when he said 'In one body we have many members, and all the members do not have the same function . . . Having gifts according to the grace given to us, let us use them . . .' and 'If the whole body were an eye, where would be the hearing? If the whole body were an ear, where would be the sense of smell?'[2] We are not required to become Baptists or Orthodox, Catholics or Anglicans—though we do number some of these in dual membership among us. Instead we are required to do and be what is peculiar to Quakers, faithfully, and in public among the other groups, even if that is uncomfortable for us and indeed others.

One of the things that is peculiar to Quakers is the ministry of silence. At the simplest level, as we have said above, Friends can share their experience of the silent framework of Meeting for Worship, and along with that their reassuring experience that quite 'ordinary' people in large numbers (a thousand or more, in London Yearly Meeting at its best) can achieve deep silence and hold it for a long period of time. They can also share, with confidence, their experience that when such human silence is achieved, the silence of God can flow through it, healing hurts and differences of every description, and making whole.

Silence carriers

The second way in which Friends might offer a ministry of silence is this: they might, as individuals empowered by the silence of God consciously experienced, offer a personal ministry of being a 'silence carrier'.

One aspect of this is the ministry of listening, and there are many (though far from enough) who offer this in a professional or trained amateur capacity—therapists, counsellors, Samaritans and others. But even that kind of listening is a long way forward from where many of us are at the moment; and listening needs to begin in our Meetings—not only, or even principally, during Meeting for Worship, lest it become what we have called Meeting for Counselling, but in our Quaker communities. Only those who have been listened to, can themselves listen.

Anyone who has spoken from their own depths in a group and been contradicted or ignored will know how painful that can feel. We all need reminding time and again that it was the religious who rushed by the man lying on the verge of the Jericho road: no doubt they were late for worthy committees on feeding the poor, or the bandit problem! The needy are not solely the inhabitants of drought-ridden countries far away (how safe it is for us when such problems are a long way off), nor even our own sick and homeless, but quite simply *anyone* who is rushed past, whose need is not heard. What is more, we are not only the priest or the Levite rushing by; we are also, each of us, lying helpless beside the road.

The ministry of the silence carrier begins, then, with the human, kindly act of paying attention to the nearest need as well as the furthest. But you do not need to be a Quaker to do this.

Silence carrying is much, much more than listening. The boundless silence of God can take into itself and heal all the cries of pain and terror there ever were or ever will be. But—just like the voice of God—the silence of God needs co-operative and experienced channels. In these circumstances it isn't that one is required to listen so much as that one would be required to take into situations of suffering and grief God's absolute silence.

An example of how this works is in helping the bereaved. Frequently the bereaved do not want answers, even when they actually ask questions about the meaning of so much suffering; and they can experience attempts at answers or explanations as frustrating if not downright offensive: no answer seems to reach the quick of their grief.

This is plainly seen in Job's anger at the 'answers' his so-called friends offer to the problem of his innocent suffering. As a matter of fact, the bible makes it abundantly clear that Job does not want answers, but healing. It is clear that God does not provide answers. First of all there is the absolute silence, then out of that a stream of images that mysteriously heals Job. Further, not even in the person of Jesus does God provide answers; only the silence and the healing images.

There is a Zen parable of a professor who went to discuss theology with a Master. He began by outlining his (very long) agenda. The Master was pouring him a cup of hospitable tea. Suddenly the professor noticed that the cup was full, even overflowing. The Master continued to pour. At last the professor could restrain himself no longer. 'Stop! The cup is overflowing! There is no room for any more tea!' The Master smiled. 'And so it is with you, my friend.'[3]

A silence carrier would take an empty cup into the world: or, better, a cup containing the silence of God.

Of course, the ability to carry the silence of God requires personal development through self-discipline and constant renewal at the source. It also requires a constant check on the ego, with its destructive private agenda ('I am famous for my silence, so I will not speak . . .'?), and it particularly needs the outward check and balance of the worshipping group. It requires frequently renewed commitment to co-operation in a difficult and at times dangerous process—so the silence-carrier needs the support group, the protective equipment, the skill. Silence-carrying will require, as T.S. Eliot says:

A condition of complete simplicity
(Costing not less than everything)[4]

One of the most telling examples of this kind of silence is given in Mark's Gospel.[5] In this description of the trial of Jesus, the teaching, arguing and talking is over. At a point in his life when most of us would have been full of arguments, persuasions and self-justification (and Pilate positively asks to be persuaded) Jesus falls silent. He now becomes overtly what he has only hinted at before: the vehicle of the absolute presence of God—not God active and creative, but God silent, imageless. It would probably have been easy for Jesus to argue his way out. But then, we would probably never have heard of him. That silence, the entry of God's silence into that terrible moment of decision, was a turning point of human history.[6]

Maybe this sounds rather grim and depressing. However, there are three things to be said about its daunting aspects. One is that it is a great deal more grim and depressing to face having refused one's calling, because that is a refusal to be oneself. The second is that responding positively to a calling releases for one the boundless creative energy of God. There will certainly be difficulties, some of them severe; but the underlying sense of what Friends call 'rightness' eventually always breaks through and somehow Pentecosts the problems. The third thing to be said is that Friends are in this together: it is a ministry to which all Friends are called in some degree.

A Ministry of Being

The third way in which Friends might offer a ministry of silence drawing upon the absolute silence of God is by recognising a calling to a ministry of being.

In one sense, a distinction between doing and being is artificial and even dangerous. For one thing, Friends align themselves all too readily in one 'camp' rather than another, finding pejorative terms for those Friends on the other 'side'. For another, as we have tried to emphasize throughout, there is ultimately no difference between doing and being. Nonetheless, when it comes to a decision about what happens *next*, what happens on Monday morning, or what happens with the sum of money actually in the bank at the moment, we do give attention to differing gifts and the differing needs into which those gifts are designed to key. Then, quite clearly, some will answer actual physical needs, offering skills in planning irrigation, or in conflict resolution, or in eye surgery, or in child care.

Some, however, will have gifts of the other kinds of healing. Friends have not yet come clear in their attitudes towards this ministry, and perhaps their ambivalence derives from their traditions, which are twofold. On the one hand they are rightly proud of their historic attention to social need, which stems directly from the gospels and from their own experience of prison, persecution, torture and alienation: there is no suggestion here that Friends should abandon their social concern—on the contrary, it is an integral part of Quaker faith. However, another part of Friends' tradition is Quietism, of which they fear a resurgence whenever there is a call for more inward search, more overt spirituality.

Quietism is regarded—not quite justly—as a period of inward-looking which led to a sectarian separation from the real world, alongside deadness in Meetings for Worship. What Friends fail sometimes to realise is that this quietism was not confined to the Religious Society of Friends, but permeated the whole early eighteenth century church in Europe as a powerful reaction against the 'enthusiasm' of the seventeenth century, which was held to have led to civil disorder and revolution. This failure to see the historical context leads Friends to blame themselves entirely for the extent to which Quietism took hold of Quakerism, and therefore to fear that Quietism is a peculiarly Quaker phenomenon. 'Being', however, is not Quietism: nothing could be less Quietist than a person who is truly 'being'.

There are already among us Friends experiencing a vocation

to a ministry of 'being for others', one example of which appears in Peter Wood's description of caring for his partner Neil (Chapter 4). We would like to see Friends who have a vocation to a ministry of being receiving encouragement and support like any other Friends with a concern, both for the sake of their own ministries (which the rest of us need very much), and for the sake of encouraging others whose sense of such a calling in themselves is not yet articulate. We would like to see lives of 'being' ministry facilitated just as lives of 'doing' ministry are. We would like to see Friends released—or even sent!—to 'be', just as Friends are presently sent to 'do'.

Of course, it is obvious (yet unfortunately needs repeating) that Friends who 'do' are also 'being': there is nothing lesser about their ministry. And it is equally obvious that a ministry of 'being' might not be wholly inactive in the material sense. But Friends would have to accept that it might be so.

An obvious example of a ministry of being is the life of Julian of Norwich, walled up in her anchorage, apparently cut off from the world and doing nothing physically but being there. Yet many found their way to her for spiritual counsel and healing; and her ministry continues to this day.

A Friend exercising a ministry of 'being' would be one of the channels into the world of God's absolute silence, a precious resource to those of us called to other ministries, and to the world which so needs the silence they offer.

*   *   *

Friends, then, would offer, as the monastic orders do, havens of silence—but out in the world, as meetings and as individuals. At the heart of this would be the renewed Meeting for Worship, where the ministry of silence and the ministry of images come together. It truly is the experience of the Religious Society of Friends that the deep silence of God is the womb of all true images. Traditional images, including treasured Quaker images, need to be taken into the absolute silence and surrendered to be tested for validity; here old images are reinfused with power and new images are forged. The artist's journey into the interior is a paradigm of this process.

In the depths of God's silence it is possible, safe, necessary, to let go of all images; and out of this letting go come power and healing. This power and healing Friends are required to share with the world.

EPILOGUE

In the Rijksmuseum in Amsterdam there is a painting by Vermeer, called *The Kitchen Maid*. A woman stands at a table, pouring milk from a jug into a bowl. On the table there are also other objects, including a basket containing a loaf of bread, and some pieces of bread lying on a cloth. We see part of a window on the left of the painting, and a plain white wall behind the woman, the wall forming at least a quarter of the whole area of the picture.

Vermeer has painted all the objects, including the woman, with loving care, indicating colour, texture, form and spatial relationships, so that we seem to feel their weight, physical reality, and relatedness. The woman is fully concentrating upon what she is doing, and this seems to draw the physical objects around her into her own meaningfulness.

Yet there are signs that Vermeer had more in his mind than setting before us a real kitchen, important though that was. The pose of the maid is that of the Virgin Mary ('Handmaid of the Lord') in mediaeval paintings, gazing down at the infant Jesus: is it coincidence that the maid is pouring milk? The maid's skirt is an intense, glowing blue achieved with lapis lazuli, one of the most expensive pigments available, and normally reserved in mediaeval art for the Virgin Mary.

Then, the pieces of bread on the table might remind us of the Feeding of the Five Thousand, and the loaf of bread in the basket of the Last Supper; and perhaps there is an echo of Jesus' saying 'I am the bread of life'. And does Vermeer intend us to think of the church's various ways of commemorating these Biblical events? Has he, thinking of priest and bread and wine, shown us instead kitchen maid, bread and milk?

By such hints and suggestions in the painting we seem to be told that for Vermeer, ordinary life was sacred, and any human act performed with attention and skill was sacramental, a kind of ministry. The painting is an image, offered from the

depth of Vermeer's vision, of the potentially sacramental nature of the physical world and everyday life in it.

There is more, yet another level of meaning. The compositional centre of the picture is the inside of the jug from which the milk is being poured. To this our eyes are frequently and questioningly drawn back from the delights of Vermeer's 'realistic' objects. The mouth of the jug is presented to our eyes as a dark space from which the milk somehow literally materialises—Vermeer gives no indication of the milk that ought to be inside the jug, although from where we 'stand' in relation to the scene we might to be able to see it. And it is from this small dark space that the utter stillness and silence of the painting emanate.

Here, then, is a ministry of images, drawn from Vermeer's ordinary, everyday experience, full of powerfully reinterpreted religious symbolism, prayerful in the silent mindfulness with which the maid performs her simple task. Vermeer communicates a 'worship seeing' of astonishing complexity, yet in very simple visual language.

Here, too, is a ministry of silence, both in what the painting says about the maid's silent attention to her work, and in the sense that her silence draws all things around her into its own frame of meaning. Her mindfulness speaks of the interconnectedness of all things. Further, the two silent areas of the painting (the jug's mouth and the white wall) are perfectly balanced, placing imagelessness at the very heart of the painting.

We see in this painting a truth about and for the Religious Society of Friends, called to a ministry of images and a ministry of silence.

REFERENCES

Full details of all books referred to here will be found in the bibliography.

Chapter 1 (pages 5–14)

1. *Luke* 10:30–35, Revised Standard Version
2. Diehl, 1991, pp.25–26
3. Vanstone, 1977
4. William Wordsworth: Lines composed a few miles above Tintern Abbey July 13 1798, II, lines 33–35
5. *Church Government:* Preamble to Chapter 24 (Ministry; eldership; oversight)
6. *Appleseed:* 'APPLESEED is a team of two Friends, Brenda Clifft Heales and Chris Cook, travelling in the ministry, with a concern to offer to Friends, in their own Meeting Houses, opportunities for learning in new ways about the spiritual journey. They seek to balance thinking and feeling modes of learning. They give short talks, which normally draw upon the Bible, Quaker writings, other faiths and the arts. Talks are followed by arts-based response activities specially designed for absolute beginners and people who do not regard themselves as 'arty'. Another important component of Appleseed days/weekends is the teaching of simple but carefully structured meditation practices.' [from Appleseed's publicity leaflet]
7. *Equipping for Ministry Conference Report:* inside cover
8. T.S. Eliot: *Preludes* [Complete Poems and Plays, p.23]
9. Isaac Penington: *The Light Within*, p.25
10. *Church Government*, para.853
11. G.M. Hopkins: *God's Grandeur* [Poems and Prose, 1963]

Chapter 2 (pages 15–25)

1. *Church Government*, para.851

2. Iris Murdoch, 1986, p.55
3. *Book of Common Prayer*, 1662, Communion Service
4. Psalm 139, Revised Authorised Version, 1982
5. *Quaker Monthly*, October 1976
6. George Fox, 1698, p.11: also in *Christian Faith and Practice*, para.406
7. Bauman, 1988, p.39
8. Robert Barclay: *Truth Triumphant*, in Bauman, op.cit. p.39
9. Bauman, op.cit., 35
10. Ibid., p.63
11. T. Edmund Harvey, in *Friends Quarterly Examiner*, 7 March 1946, p.191
12. Bauman, op.cit., p.130
13. George Fox, *Journal* (Epistle to Friends), pp.283–4
14. Francis Hall, 1984, pp.52, 67

Chapter 3 (pages 29–46)

1. P.W. Martin, 1955, pp.115, 240
2. Dr. Seuss, 1940
3. Wordsworth, *Tintern Abbey*, II, lines 93–99
4. T.S. Eliot: *Four Quartets*, Burnt Norton, in 1969, p.175
5. *Exodus* 3:2–5 Revised Standard Version
6. John Keats: *Ode on a Grecian Urn*
7. T.S. Eliot, op.cit., p.175
8. See footnote for Chapter 1, no.6
9. T.S. Eliot, op. cit., p.190
10. Gaus, 1988, p.185
11. T.S. Eliot, op.cit., p.175
12. *The Friend*, 5 February 1988, pp.133–4
13. George Herbert, 1963, p.13.
14. A Zen koan is a riddle or paradox given to students of Zen to work upon until they have exhausted all possible logical answers. At that point they become open to true insight and enlightenment.

15. Marion Milner, 1971, p.162
16. Janet Martin Soskice, 1985, p.66
17. Ibid., p.140
18. T.S. Eliot, op.cit., p.175

Chapter 4 (pages 47–62)

1. Lionel Blue: *Back Door to Heaven*, p.11
2. William Wordsworth: 'The world is too much with us' (Sonnet 33) in *Miscellaneous Sonnets*.

Note: All quotations from Julian of Norwich in this chapter rendered in modern English have been translated by Brenda Clifft Heales. Page reference are to the mediæval text, but chapter numbers are also given to facilitate finding the quotations in any of the modern translations which appear in the bibliography. The mediæval text used was: Julian of Norwich: *A Revelation of Love*, ed. Marion Glasscoe, 1976

3. Op.cit., Chapter 75, p.91
4. Ibid., Chapter 40, p.42
5. Ibid., Chapter 27, p.29
6. Ibid., Chapter 2, p.2
7. Ibid., Chapter 16, p.18
8. Ibid., Chapter 17, p.20
9. Ibid., Chapter 19, p.21
10. Ibid., Chapter 21, p.23
11. Ibid., Chapter 7, p.8
12. Ibid., Chapter 6, p.7
13. Ibid., Chapter 57, p.68: 'For the higher part of our nature is knitted to God in its creation and God is knitted to the lower part as we take on our bodies; thus in Christ our two natures are united.'
14. Ibid., Chapter 10, p.11
15. Ibid., Chapter 5, pp.5–6
16. Ibid., Chapter 42, p.44

17. Ibid., Chapter 56, p.67
18. Ibid., Chapter 86, p.102

Chapter 5 (pages 65–82)
1. See especially the Athanasian Creed
2. Pseudo-Dionysius: *The Mystical Theology* in *Complete Works*, 1987, p.135
3. Smith, 1987, p.25
4. See Walshe, 1987
5. A.A. Milne, 1926, p.67
6. A version of this story can be found in Blue, 1985, p.40

Chapter 6 (pages 83–88)
1. George Fox, *Journal*, p.19 also in *Christian Faith and Practice*, para.7
2. Clark & Skinner, 1958, p.226 (Eckhart's Commentary on the Book of Exodus)
3. George Fox, 1698, p.11 also in *Christian Faith and Practice*, para.406

Chapter 7 (pages 91–104)
1. Francis Hall, 1984, p.78
2. Ibid., p.76
3. Ibid., p.71
4. Genesis 1:2 RSV
5. S.T. Coleridge: *Biographia Literaria*, Ch. 13, p.167
6. Coleridge: *Frost at Midnight*
7. Shakespeare: *A Midsummer Night's Dream*, V, 1, 12–17
8. Cecil Collins—a retrospective exhibition: catalogue, 1989, p.37
9. George Gorman, 1973, p.31
10. Iris Murdoch, TV interview, published in *Revelations: Glimpses of Reality*, 1985; pp.88–9

11. G.M. Hopkins: *Poems and Prose*, 1953, pp.145–6
12. Isaac Penington: *The Light Within*, pp.21, 25
13. Appleseed: see footnote 6, Chapter 1
14. Friends who would like more information about setting up such activities in their own meetings could see Cook & Heales, 1989
15. *To Lima with Love*, 1987, para.37, p.10
16. John Keats, *Letters*, 1954, p.80. Keats' actual words were 'budding patiently under the eye of Apollo'
17. See Chapter 3, pp.44
18. Isaac Penington: op.cit., p.29
19. Ann & Barry Ulanov, 1985, ix
20. Isaac Penington: op.cit., p.36
21. From Testimony to the Life of Anne Whitehead, in *Piety Promoted*, 1686, quoted in Quaker Women's Group, 1986, p.14
22. *Gifts and Discoveries* Three-phase study pack, jointly published by Quaker Home Service and Woodbrooke, 1987+
23. *John* 10:10 RSV

Chapter 8 (pages 105–116)

1. *Equipping for Ministry Conference Report*, 1990, p.53
2. *Romans* 12:4,6; I *Corinthians* 12:17 both RSV
3. See Paul Reps, 1971, p.17
4. T.S. Eliot, *Four Quartets*, in *Complete Poems and Plays*, p.198
5. *Mark* 15:1–5
6. See also W.H. Vanstone, 1982—a marvellous study of the way in which Jesus passed from teaching to silence—though Vanstone interprets the meaning of the silence rather differently.

BIBLIOGRAPHY

The bibliography includes all the books for which we have given footnotes; and some others for further reading.

William Anderson: *Cecil Collins—the quest for the great happiness*, Barrie and Jenkins, London, 1988

Richard Bauman: *Let Your Words Be Few*, Cambridge U.P., 1983.

Jonathan Baylis: *Gerald Manley Hopkins—portrait of a poet* (has an accompanying video-tape), The Picture Publishing Co., London, 1989

Lionel Blue: *Back Door to Heaven*, Harper/Collins, London, 1985

Bright Blue, B.B.C. Publications, London, 1985

Christopher Bryant: *The River Within*, Darton, Longman and Todd, London, 1978

Christian Faith and Practice in the Experience of the Religious Society of Friends, London Yearly Meeting, London, 1966

Church Government, London Yearly Meeting, London, 1968

James M. Clark & John V. Skinner (Trans. & eds.): *Meister Eckhart—Selected Treatises and Sermons*, Faber and Faber, London 1958

S.T. Coleridge: *Biographia Literaria* (ed. George Watson), Everyman, London, 1956

Chris Cook & Brenda Heales: *Meeting for Art*, London, 1989

Oliver Davies (trans. & ed.): *The Rhineland Mystics—an anthology*, SPCK, London, 1989

Oliver Davies: *Meister Eckhart: Mystical Theologian*, SPCK, London 1991. (Note: published since this book was written—see specially Chapter 8 on Eckhart's Language)

William H. Diehl: *The Monday Connection*, Harper, San Francisco, 1991

Betty Edwards: *Drawing on the Artist Within*, Fontana, London, 1988

Drawing on the Right Side of the Brain, Fontana, London, 1979

Equipping for Ministry Conference Report, QHS and Woodbrooke, Birmingham, 1990

T.S. Eliot: *The Complete Poems and Plays*, Faber and Faber, London, 1969

Robert K.C. Forman: *Meister Eckhart—the Mystic as Theologian*, Element, Shaftesbury, 1991

George Fox: *A Collection of ... Epistles*, London, 1698

George Fox: *Journal*, ed. John L. Nickalls, Cambridge, 1952. U.P., reprinted by London Yearly Meeting 1975.

Andy Gaus: *The Unvarnished Gospels*, Element, Shaftsbury, 1988.

George Gorman: *The Amazing Fact of Quaker Worship*, Quaker Home Service, London, 1973

Francis B. Hall: *Practical Spirituality*, ed. Howard Alexander and others, author's estate, Richmond (Indiana), 1984

F.C. Happold: *Mysticism—a study and an anthology*, Penguin, Harmondsworth, 1970

George Herbert: Selected by David Herbert, Vista Books, London 1963

Gerard Manley Hopkins: *Poems and Prose*, Penguin, London, 1963

Grace M. Jantzen: *Julian of Norwich—mystic and theologian*, SPCK, London, 1987

Julian of Norwich: *Revelations of Divine Love*, ed. Halcyon Backhouse & Rhona Pipe, Hodder and Stoughton, London, 1987

Showings, trans./ed. E. Colledge & J. Walsh, Paulist Press, New York, 1978

A Revelation of Love, ed. Marion Glasscoe, University of Exeter, 1976

Revelations of Divine Love, trans./ed. Clifton Wolters, Penguin, Harmondsworth, 1966

Rufus Jones: *Some Exponents of Mystical Religion*, Epworth Press, London, 1930

John Keats: *Letters*, selected by Frederick Page, Oxford University Press, London, 1954

Robert Llewelyn: *With Pity not with Blame—the spirituality of Julian of Norwich and The Cloud of Unknowing for Today*, Darton Longman and Todd, London, 1989

Andrew Louth: *Denys the Areopagite*, Chapman, London, 1989

P.W. Martin: *Experiment in Depth*, Routledge and Kegan Paul, London, 1955

A.A. Milne: *Winnie-the-Pooh*, Methuen, London 1926

Marion Milner (Joanna Field): *A Life of One's Own* (1934), Virago, London, 1986

An Experiment in Leisure (1937), Virago, London, 1986

On Not Being Able to Paint, Heinemann, London, 1971

Iris Murdoch: in *Revelations: Glimpses of Reality*, ed. Ronald S. Wells, Shepheard-Walwyn, Routledge and Kegan Paul, London, 1985

The Sovereignty of Good, London, 1970

Brant Pelphrey: *Christ Our Mother—Julian of Norwich*, Darton Longman and Todd, London, 1989

Isaac Penington: *The Light Within and Selected Writings*, Tract Association of Friends, Philadelphia, no date, but 20thC

Pseudo-Dionysius: *The Complete Works*, SPCK, London, 1987

Quaker Women's Group: *Bringing the Invisible into the Light*, Quaker Home Service, London, 1986

Paul Reps: *Zen Flesh, Zen Bones*, Penguin, Harmondsworth, 1971

Isabel Ross: *Margaret Fell—Mother of Quakerism*, Sessions, York, 1984

Nancy Roth: *The Breath of God—an approach to prayer*, Cowley, Cambridge (Massachusetts), 1990

Dr. Seuss: *Horton Hatches the Egg* (1940), Collins, London, 1962

Cyprian Smith: *The Way of Paradox—spiritual life as taught by Meister Eckhart*, Darton Longman and Todd, London, 1987

Janet Martin Soskice: *Metaphor and Religious Language*, Oxford University Press, London, 1985

Thich Nhat Hanh: *Being Peace*, Parallax Press, Berkeley (California), 1987

Frank Tobin: *Meister Eckhart: thought and language*, University of Pennsylvania Press, Philadelphia, 1986

To Lima with Love—Baptism, Eucharist and Ministry: a Quaker Response, London Yearly Meeting, London, 1987

Ann & Barry Ulanov: *Primary Speech—a psychology of prayer*, SCM Press, London, 1982

Sheila Upjohn: *In Search of Julian of Norwich*, Darton Longman and Todd, London, 1989

W.H. Vanstone: *Love's Endeavour, Love's Expense*, Darton Longman and Todd, London, 1977
The Stature of Waiting, Darton Longman and Todd, London, 1982

M. O'C. Walshe (trans. & ed.): *Meister Eckhart: Sermons and treatises* (3 volumes), Element, Shaftesbury, 1987

Richard Woods: *Eckhart's Way*, Darton Longman and Todd, London, 1987